DISCARDED

ANATOMY OF THE
HOT ROD

Doug Mitchel

©2007 Doug Mitchel
Published by

krause publications
An Imprint of F+W Publications

700 East State Street • Iola, WI 54990-0001
715-445-2214 • 888-457-2873
www.krausebooks.com

Our toll-free number to place an order or obtain
a free catalog is (800) 258-0929.

Library of Congress Catalog Number: 2006935764

ISBN 13-digit: 978-0-89689-450-1

Designed by Kara Grundman
Edited by John Gunnell

Printed in China

DEDICATION

To Frank Peiler

For igniting the spark of enthusiasm for all things automotive when
I was a kid, and fanning the flames ever since.

SPECIAL THANKS

Special thanks goes to the shops, car owners and the entire hot rod community for taking time out of their hectic schedules so I could photograph their four-wheeled artwork. Of the many people involved, I must express a special thanks to the following:

Brian and George, otherwise known as "Kevin and Greg," at Felony Chops and Rodz for exposing me to an entirely different way of building hot rods.

Terry Getzelman and the crew at Getz's Hot Rod Innovations for rolling out some of their fantastic customs and subjecting them to my photography.

Bill Jelinek at Route 66 Motorsports for taking time away from his many endeavors and allowing me to photograph some of his automotive sculpture.

Tim O'Connell of O'Connell Specialties fame, for both building some spectacular cars and introducing me to their owners.

James Talaga for opening the doors to his private collection and providing me with an entire day to shoot some of his hot rods.

Dan Ulreich and the team at Midwest Hot Rods for repeatedly making their shop my home as I dragged one car after another in front of my lens.

CONTENTS

INTRODUCTION

The times they are a-changin'.

In the infancy of this hobby, hot rods could be easily grouped into neat categories. The categories were determined by the purists and hard-core rodders. As time marches on, the definitions of a "hot rod" has morphed into almost anything the owner wants it to be. I suppose a Yugo with chrome spinners may be pushing the envelope a bit, but who's to say that guy is wrong for doing what makes him happy? As I see it, that is the key factor when building a hot rod to fill the space in your garage.

As you read through this book, you'll find stories ranging from decade long build-ups to cars that were simply purchased to fill a void. Regardless of which path was taken, the end result is another proud owner of an amazing car. It seems to be that the state of the union is just that, any car that is customized, driven and shown with pride can fall into the hot rod guidelines. Big engines, flashy paint and tuck and roll interiors don't hurt, though.

Of course the purists may complain that we have opened the velvet ropes to let any guy with a car into the exclusive club, but in reality, it was always that way. The limiting factor in the early days was the pool of cars that was available to customize and the lack of any aftermarket parts.

When the craze began, cars were still considered to be tools that were needed to get around. The majority of car owners used their vehicles to get to work, earn a living and carry their families to gatherings and events. To simply use a luxury like a car as a toy to be altered for mere pleasure seemed a crime. Of course there were always those without the family obligations and the freedom to do what they desired with their autos. These pioneers and their creative minds set the wheels of hot rodding into motion, and they haven't stopped rolling yet.

Not only could they envision the car of their dreams but were also fully capable of hammering them to life—bending, painting and bolting their way into history. From this initial crush came some names that still ring true in the hall of fame and inspire others to follow their paths. There have been some slowdowns in the field, but all major trends are cyclical in nature. The fact of the matter is hot rods have been a passion for a growing number of people for the past five decades. They offer an ever-expanding pool of talent and options.

Anyone with the desire and enough extra cash can put together a car that fills his or her needs. There are no rules, guidelines or regulations telling us what a car must or cannot be, and even the small sampling shown on these pages illustrates the vast variety rolling around the streets of this country.

Once the decision is made, all that needs to be addressed are the requirements, costs and time frame. Seeing as to how many catalogs, hot rod shops and bone yards exist today, there should be no reason why anyone with the passion to own one shouldn't be behind the wheel. We may not have invented the wheel, but our demand to drive around in really cool ones is a great direction to go.

Whether you choose the suede black rat rod or glossy red high-end roadster matters not. Just build what you like and let the world admire your efforts. I know I will.

1965 FORD MUSTANG

Owners: Allen Utacht
Builder: Midwest Hot Rods/Paul Quinn,
Randy Schwartz, Dan Ulreich

As a long-time fan of the '65 and '66 Mustangs, the owner of this car decided to show the world what could be done to a classic "pony car." His opinion was they were often overlooked and hoped to change that with this build.

Wanting to upgrade a classic car like the Mustang takes some finesse in order not to destroy the terrific lines of the original design while more contemporary alterations are applied. When the owner decided to have this car created, he turned to Midwest Hot Rods, knowing that their well-earned reputation for building high-end cars would not disappoint.

At first glance, the car appears to be almost unaltered in its stance and shape, but a closer examination tells a different story. Beginning with the front valance, we find all new contours that were shaped from steel, not your typical fiberglass. The hand-formed front air dam blends gracefully into the arched wheel flares that lead the eyes to the curvaceous rocker panels.

Each of the dual exhaust outlets finds its perfectly formed opening in the steel panels. The rear wheel wells also get accented with an arch of sheet metal. The tail section includes another wide range of alterations including a bumper that has been moved inboard by an inch. The back-up lights, fuel-fill door and license plate have been mounted flush to the skin keeping a tidy appearance. The subtle three-sided rear spoiler is also crafted from steel and adds the perfect degree of aerodynamic contour to the stubby deck lid.

Retaining a classic feature of a 1960s-era Thunderbird, the turn signal bulbs flash sequentially when activated. Lighting the way at night is a pair of halogen headlamps that have the turn signals integrated into their design. Even more light can be cast from the large diameter halogen driving lights mounted in the lower grille opening. Additional bits of custom metal on the outside of the car include the three sets of air scoops that are found on the hood, rear quarter and sail panels. All of this sheet metal was created by Dan and was more evidence of his talents.

Dan Ulreich of Midwest Hot Rod fame wasn't content to simply create an exterior that bristled with fresh contours, but continued his efforts under the hood. Eighteen-gauge metal was the choice to form the firewall and inner fender walls. That created an engine compartment as sleek as the rest of the Mustang.

In his efforts to sterilize the engine bay Dan removed the vertical shock towers, resulting in a smooth sweep of steel on each side of the space. Covering every inch of the reshaped sheet metal is Silver Effect Pearl paint from Spies Hecker contrasted with Charcoal Effect Pearl from the same maker.

Now that we find ourselves under the hood, we can discuss the motivation for this rod. Nestled in the motor mounts we find a Ford 351 Windsor mill that has been massaged to produce 480 horsepower. In the factory trim, this same motor only churned out about 248 ponies, so we can see how this updated mill has been improved. Assembled by Fast Times Motorworks, Inc., the lump is carbureted by a Holley 750-cfm, double pump unit and fed with an electric fuel pump. A triangular, billet aluminum air cleaner rests atop the carburetor and provides a free flow of air while grabbing dirt and debris before it can reach the intake.

Hammering out 480 horsepower from the 351 Windsor motor, the V-8 delivers plenty of performance from its sterile surroundings.

The large red button serves as the method of starting the car, and the high-end electronics from Alpine and MTX deliver concert quality sound.

Another bit of Dan's handiwork is the vents found on each of the Mustang's sail panels.

Also formed from sheet metal are the intake vents and the gentle curves of the rocker panels complete with exhaust outlets that match the chrome tips perfectly.

Crafted from steel, the front fascia blends smoothly into the fenders and integrates cleanly with the lower chin spoiler and bumper. The Halogen headlights illuminate the road and incorporate powerful turn signal bulbs. The hoodscoops, bent from raw sheet metal, are beautiful and functional.

Street & Performance supplied the pulleys that keep the serpentine belt in place and add another touch of glamour to the underhood compartment. An aluminum radiator keeps the temperature under control, no matter how hot the action gets. Leading spent fumes away from the motor is an exhaust system formed from 2-1/2-inch diameter stainless steel tubing running under the chassis and exiting through the hand-bent rocker panels.

A pair of Flowmaster mufflers lies between the motor and the tandem outlets to tame the racket coming from the potent mill. The resulting tone is mellow, yet sounds anxious to be uncorked. The five-speed manual gearbox puts the proper ratios in the owner's hand, and brings more of the old-world charm to the build.

Retaining the factory Mustang chassis, the running gear was modified with a Heidt's cross member teamed with tubular control arms and coil springs. Moser was selected for the rear suspension and the nine-inch rear end is complete with Positraction. Slowing this sleek Mustang down from speed are Wilwood calipers and drilled rotors at all four corners. No sense in going fast if you can't stop. Seventeen-inch Nitto rubber keeps the Intro brand, 17-inch rims off the tarmac with 225/45s up front and 225/50s on the rear

hoops. Each of the rims was also powder coated in the same Charcoal Effect Pearl used on the racing stripes to complete the circuit.

Inside the silver '65 is a custom interior built by Midwest Hot Rods. Both front seats, as well as the rear, were custom formed before being swaddled in black leather. The door panels were also created for this car from scratch, showing us the range of talents available at the Midwest shop. The center console is another bit of one-off handiwork that brings a new level of comfort to this very driveable hot rod. Additional vents were added to the dashboard, along with HVAC controls and a push-button start.

Wrapped in more black leather is the billet aluminum steering wheel that lives at the end of a tilt column. A complete set of gauges from VDO keep the driver up to date on velocity, rpms and pertinent pressures and temperatures. Power windows and steering bring more ease of use to the equation, and an Alpine sound system is mated to amplified MTX speakers and sub-woofer.

The completed project looks as great as it runs, and it runs very well, indeed. Melding old and new has never looked so good, but comes as no surprise when Midwest Hot Rods turns their attention to a new design.

The Thunderbird taillights, the fuel door and license plate are all flush-mounted and the rear bumper has been moved inward by one inch to complete the concept.

"LA RATA"

Owner and Builder: John "Stitch" Benauides

When hot rodding was in its infancy, people who wanted to own one of these newfangled cars had to build it themselves. Using whatever vehicle was available and affordable as a platform, the work could begin. Any desired changes to the body, motor and interior were created and completed by the owner and maybe a few buddies on the weekend. High-end hot rod shops and catalogs full of shiny billet components were not even an idea at that stage of the game, so each individual's creativity was put to the test. The cars built in the day were only the beginning of what we could expect as the years rolled by.

Along with the major builders of today's best hot rods, there is again a movement by the home builder to create and assemble cars with whatever materials and talents are on hand. Earning the nickname of "rat rods," these vehicles have earned a place in the hearts of many hot rod enthusiasts and possess a charm all their own.

Seeing this trend expanding, the owner of "La Rata" decided he wanted to build one of his own. As a long-time owner of a custom automotive upholstery shop, he had seen all manners of hot rods roll into his shop. Once the decision was made to build his personal rat rod, the work began with the most basic of elements and grew from that point on.

Not content to retain the stock windshield visor, "Stitch" modified it by adding the ventilation.

"Stitch" wanted his car to be long and lean, so he began work by building his own chassis. Steel tubing that measured 1-1/8 x 3 inches was chosen, and the 3/16-inch thickness of the material would provide adequate rigidity for the lengthy design he had in mind.

The body of "La Rata" began life as a 1929 Ford Model A, two-door sedan, and was then chopped five inches and channeled three inches. These alterations allowed the roofline to fit the now-revised mounting location of the body on the frame. Additional bits of custom sheet metal can be seen in the perforated windshield visor and peaked air cleaner cover. The new dimensions of the shell required fresh glass to be installed and safety laminated panels to fill the

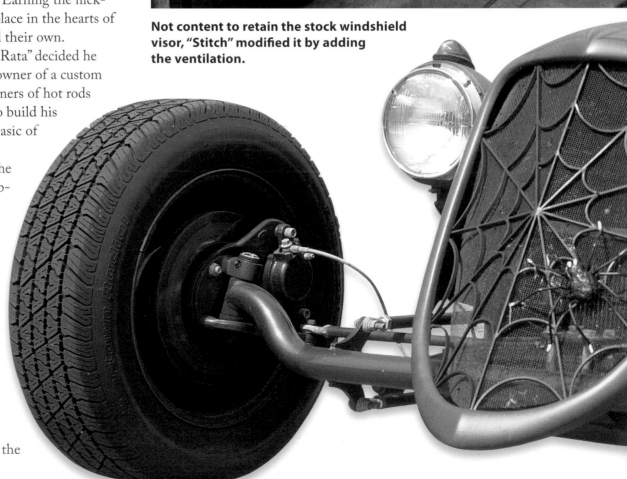

voids. Once completed, the body was "finished" in a combination of rust and green painted trim.

In harsh contrast to some of the beautiful interiors he has created for clients, the cockpit of "La Rata" is devoid of any trim or even the most basic of upholstery. The modified Corvette seats are wrapped with nothing more than slipcovers and a pair of VooDoo Kings t-shirts for protection. The steering wheel was a local junkyard find that had originally turned the wheels of a Chevrolet. When compared to the stark nature of the interior, the 300-watt stereo, complete with a set of 10-inch woofers, seems out of place, but a man must have his music.

Of course any hot rod worth its salt will have an impressive power plant and "La Rata" is no different, having borrowed a 1954 Chrysler Hemi that displaces 331 cubic inches. Some 235 horsepower is on tap and the mill is fed through four matching Stromberg 48 carbs on a rare Horne manifold. Each of the four Strombergs has its own two-inch round air cleaner to keep the debris at bay. Feeding the family of four is an electric fuel pump that draws from a 16-gallon reservoir.

Handling the exhaust is a pair of 105-mm artillery shells that are mated to the handmade headers. Creative usage of surplus military hardware is probably the truest form of a real hot rod since the first

Two-inch whitewalls are mated with a set of Lancer hub caps for the best in old-world details.

Altering a pair of Corvette seats for use, "Stitch" added only slipcovers and a pair of t-shirts for upholstery.

For a touch of whimsy, the radiator shroud has been accessorized with a spider web and the spider himself.

A 331-cid Chrysler Hemi gives this Old-World iron New World power. Each carb has its own air cleaner, but a hood over them keeps water out. It's rare to see four carbs on a modern rod — especially four Strombergs. War surplus 105-mm artillery shells serve as collectors for the homemade headers.

VOODOO KINGS

The rear bumper was pirated from a `57 Caddy, then shortened and flipped upside down.

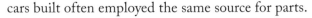

cars built often employed the same source for parts.

A Chevrolet Turbo 400 transmission offers up three speeds and feeds the resulting ratio to the Ford nine-inch rear end, complete with Positraction for control. Air bags bring a level of comfort to the ride and offer some adjustability in the ride height as well. Keeping things cool is a radiator from a 1937 Chevrolet, cut down to size for use in this rod. The cowl for the radiator has been modified with a combination of mesh, and a handcrafted spider's web, complete with a large arachnid, clinging to the surface. The application of components from nearly every major automotive source is another true hot rod element, with no boundaries between makes and models being harvested for parts.

Coker brand, Silvertown tires roll at every corner with the appropriate two-inch white walls adding a touch of luxury to the overall appearance. Steel wheels measuring five inches up front and eight inches out back are trimmed with Lancer hubcaps for the sake of dazzle. The front end consists of a standard four-inch dropped axle with 36-inch radius rods. A disc brake system, taken from a contemporary General Motors car, graces each front wheel while large drum brakes are installed on the rear.

Lighting on "La Rata" is what we'd expect, with a pair of Mack truck headlight buckets up front. The rear bumper is actually a front bumper from a 1957 Cadillac that has been narrowed to 24 inches, then flipped upside-down before being attached to the frame. Turn signal lamps have been converted from trailer lights for simplicity and brightness.

So how long does it take a person to build a rat rod of this nature? It took "Stitch" about seven months for the complete assembly, doing 99 percent of the work himself. The Hemi motor was rebuilt by Milo, and the distributor required some outside service as well. Everything else was up to "Stitch," and he's proud of that feat. He is a member of the VooDoo Kings, a club where modern hot rods are not allowed. "La Rata" fits the club's rules and regulations to the letter.

While "La Rata" (translation: "the rat") may not win any wards for best paint or interior, it is the dictionary definition for a modern day "rat rod." Taking his own vision and building a car from the parts available, John has fulfilled his duty as a rat rod home builder.

1941 WILLYS

Owner: Tom Clinton
Builder: Midwest Hot Rods/
Dan Quinn, Randy Schwarz, Dan Ulreich

With a heritage dating back to 1912 Willys-Overland, the luxurious and powerful Willys-Knight, and the more famous Willys Jeep, the Willys brand of cars survived in America from 1933 to 1963. It then faded into automotive history like many other once thriving nameplate. The late 1930s and early '40s Willy models have become favorites among the hot rod clan. Often run as drag racing machines, otherwise known as "gassers," the swooping bodywork has also been integrated into a number of street legal cars.

Examples of true, steel-bodied Willys are becoming quite scarce and expensive these days, but a number of aftermarket fiberglass reproductions are available. This allows an owner to create the look of the original car without the worry of ruining one of the few remaining steel Willys models on the street. The skin on this example hails from the Outlaw Performance catalog and makes for a terrific starting point for the builder. Although capable of being assembled in a residential garage setting, this 1941 was built by Midwest Hot Rods in Plainfield, Illinois. We'll see several of their expansive range of creations in this book.

The owner selected to have his Willys carry a "suicide" style hood that flipped forward when opened. This is not normally a big deal. The shell of the Outlaw front end lacks any rigid structure beneath it. This is not a flaw, but simply a way to provide the builder with a myriad of methods to mount the front end of his own car. Before being able to attach the husk to the chassis, Dan Ulreich of Midwest had to construct a structural skeleton to carry the lid. Once the front clip was reinforced, the entire assembly was enclosed within another layer of hand-laid fiberglass for an impressively sterile appearance. Hot rod owners and builders are quite concerned with every facet of their cars, both open and closed.

Once the front clip is tilted into its open position we find an enormous 540-cubic inch engine from Donovan, built by Lingenfelter Performance Engineering. Not knowing when to leave well enough alone, the owner opted for a BDS blower and fuel injection system to feed the massive mill. The results of these efforts produce

The alloy dashboard makes no bones about being all business, and the lack of audio system confirms its intentions.

Mounted to the floor is this mechanical device used to shift the car between any of the three forward speeds with no muss or fuss.

Mounted to the top of the massive motor is the drag racing style intake with red butterflies that allow air to rush into the blower on command.

a horsepower number somewhere north of 1,200, enough for any speed freak, on-track or off. Needing a clear path to exhale, the engine has been fitted with exhaust headers that were hand bent by Midwest using 3-1/2-inch diameter stainless steel. Hoping to corral some of the racket is a pair of stainless steel mufflers.

Power is fed into a 400 automatic transmission with a manual shift body, encapsulating the best of both worlds. The floor-mounted shifter from Precision Performance Products lacks any exotic leather boot or comfortable shift knob, and looks all business. The chosen gear ratio is then

delivered via a Ford nine-inch rear end that has been narrowed to fit within the Willys fenders. With a set of rear donuts measuring 15 inches across, we can see why the rear axle had to be truncated for use. E.T. five-spoke wheels are found at all four corners, and were

The front nose of the Willys has been cosmetically purified and features flush mount headlights and a tubular, horizontal grille.

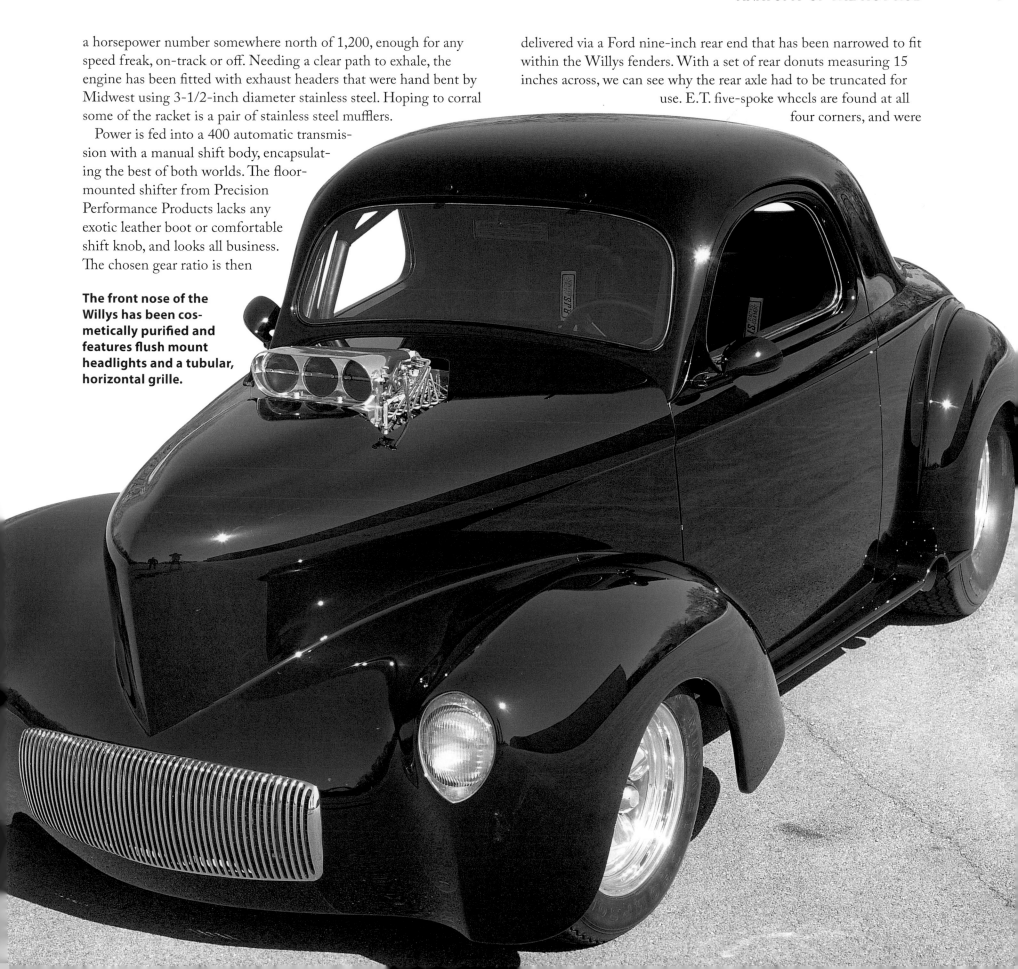

polished to within an inch of their lives before getting the Mickey Thompson rubber stretched over their beads.

While straight-line performance is the strong point for this Willys, it has been equipped with plenty of cornering gear too. Up front we find independent suspension with tubular control arms and a set of coil-over shocks. The entire assembly has also been polished to a gleaming luster. An equally polished four-bar suspension does its

The Outlaw chassis is as clean as the body it holds in place, and the license plate frame flips out of view when the car is not running.

best to keep the big meats under control during hard acceleration and cornering. Wilwood brakes are installed on each wheel to provide the required stopping power. All of the required running gear and drive train are mounted to an Outlaw Performance chassis.

The Outlaw fiberglass body has been highly modified for use on this car, and again shows us the talents of the builders at Midwest Hot Rods. The headlights have been molded into the curves of the front fenders while a pair of oval taillights and the mandatory third brake light has also been faired into the skin.

The drive belt for the BDS blower hides behind a small cowling that was created to smooth out the lines of the hood assembly. Steel running boards are employed to add some rigidity to the body and look great, too. Small openings for the exiting exhaust were formed into the metal instead of simply dropping the pipes lower, a beautiful bit of extra effort that looks right at home. Once the bodywork was completed, Spies Hecker Dark Candy Apple Purple was applied to the entire surface, and then rubbed to a high gloss.

The interior of this 1941 Willys has not been overlooked, and it provides both comfort and safety for this street legal race car. Two seats taken from a late model Lincoln were used to create the deeply bolstered saddles we now see, and black leather covers their contours. Massive, four-point racing harnesses have replaced the standard chest and waist belts used on most vehicles. The same black leather was used on the door panels with purple accents to break up the acres of dark hides.

The dashboard was crafted from aluminum, and then ball milled and polished to create the machined surface. A comprehensive set of Auto Meter gauges keep the driver apprised of the car's every activity, pressure and temperature. The steering wheel is another polished aluminum feature with a black leather wrap for comfort and grip. Another testament to the car's intentions is the 10-point steel roll cage that ensconces the driver and passenger. Not only does this assembly help to add stiffness to the chassis, but it would prove invaluable in keeping the occupants safe in the event of a rollover crash. One item you won't find in the modern Willys build is a radio or sound system of any kind. The music of the 540-cid engine coursing through the enormous exhaust will have to provide

any music to your ears. To hear the sound even better, the windows roll down with the touch of the electric switch.

Although the Willys nameplate may not be as ubiquitous as Ford or Chevy, its design and heritage are shown with pride in this modern day version of a classic.

Displacing 540 cubic inches, this engine from Donovan was built to racing specs by Lingenfelter Performance Engineering and puts out more than 1,200 horsepower.

1933 FORD PICKUP

Owner: Jake Schwarz
Builder: Jake and Randy Schwarz

Having spent many years attending car shows with his father, Randy, Jake knew that one day he'd build one of his own. It's tough to escape the draw of hot rodding when your dad is up to his ears in the business of building them, and Jake didn't even try to loosen the bonds. Inspiration for this specific project came after seeing a California-built, 1934 Ford truck crafted by Jimmy Shrine. Combining that desire with the passion instilled by his father, Jake set off to begin the creation of his own custom truck.

With a clear idea of what his hot rod truck would look like, Jake set out to collect the required hardware. Being a true hot rod, no limits were placed on the sources of the components required for the final assembly. Along with bits and pieces from a variety of manufacturers, the truck is chock full of handmade parts and assemblies. An entire year was needed to complete the job, but Jake wasn't in a rush to fulfill his dream.

The donor chassis was taken from a 1933 Ford half-ton pickup truck, and it was partially boxed for added strength. This process entails welding a fourth wall of steel to the "C" channel of an existing frame. The resulting boxed structure is much stronger than the factory design, and adds another dimension of "custom" to any build.

The cab of the truck was found in less than perfect condition, with the lower section rotted away from years of neglect. Jake shaped sections of flat steel using an English wheel to re-create the gentle contours of the lower sections of the cab, doors and cowling. To further aid in his custom look, the newly formed cab and doors were channeled by 7-1/2 inches to sit lower on the frame rails. The radiator cowling was sectioned by 3 inches and channeled by 4-1/2 inches to better match the fresh profile of the rest of the body.

A truck bed from a 1935 Ford, was channeled by 7-1/2 inches and shortened by six inches. Needing a new floor for the revamped bed, Jake took a flat sheet of steel, and then used a bead roller to add ribs for added rigidity. This amount of custom bodywork is tedious and time consuming, but sets a real hot rod apart from the crowd.

For added drama, a "suicide" front end was chosen for the build. This design put the axle out in front of the frame rails, suspended by hand-created brackets and hardware. The four-inch dropped axle was drilled for appearance and holds wheels and brakes taken from a 1940 Ford in place.

The 6 x 16-inch B. F. Goodrich Silvertown tires were chosen for their retro look and safe driving characteristics. Beneath the truncated truck bed we find a Posie monoleaf suspension arrangement with more brakes and wheels from a 1940 Ford. Slightly wider 7.50 x 16-inch Firestone rubber was spooned onto the rims. The steel wheels are painted bright red with a set of "dog dish" wheel covers for a touch of flash.

Power for the truck is based on a 289-cubic-inch mill stolen from a 1965 Ford. The small-block V-8 is fed by a four-barrel carb and manual fuel pump. A period Cal Custom air cleaner filters out the debris while more 1965 Ford parts are listed under the "pulley" and "radiator" columns. The power is sent to a 1940 Ford banjo rear end before reaching the drive tires. A set of nerf bars formed from ¾-inch steel tubing hold the pumpkin in its place.

Because of the custom dimensions of the truck's body and bed, a hand-formed exhaust systemwas required to lead the spent gases away.

Beginning at the block, a set of handmade headers begin the journey.

The primary collector tubes are fitted with cutouts in the event, an extra measure of free breathing is required. Leaving the cutout caps in place sends the fumes southward through a set of "lime fires" leading into a set of "belly burners." After traveling under the cab of the truck, the pipes again appear and climb to the upper lip of the bed where they take a hard 90-degree turn and head for the tail section. Mufflers are little more than sections of straight pipe, so sound reduction is minimal at best.

Inside the cab we find a fairly austere combination of upholstery and raw steel. A set of seats taken from a Dodge Caravan were re-covered in pleated vinyl as were the inside door panels. A colorful blanket is thrown over the vinyl for just the right look. Jake and his dad, Randy, are the men credited with the stitch work. Modern Stewart-Warner gauges were installed into the 1933 Ford dashboard, and a steering column from a 1940 Ford was shortened and u-jointed in three places to make the tortuous journey between steering wheel and steering box.

Snaking under the truck's cab and reappearing to travel
the high road, the "belly burner" exhaust is pure hot rod.

Made from scratch, the headers feature removable cutouts that allow for a quick boost in power and noise.

A vintage Cal Custom air cleaner looks right at home on this retro-rod.

A "necker's knob" adorns the steering wheel while a flamed shift knob makes another nice touch to the interior's design.

A 289-cubic-inch engine moves the 1933 Ford along smartly without being abusive.

The painted steering wheel was also purloined from a 1940 Ford and mated with a "necker's knob," a popular accessory of the day. The cue ball-sized shift knob sits atop a lengthy lever that reaches high up into the cockpit.

The lever and knob are used to select one of three gears within the C-4 transmission. Simple wooden roof panels keep the rain out of the cabin, and glass from a 1933 model was tinted gray to keep the heat down to a minimum.

The exterior finish began with a coat of Rally Matte Black from PPG. Bill "Jive" Jarvis applied pinstriping and graphics for a touch of Old-World hot rod. For night driving, a pair of aftermarket headlamps were installed up front and a matching set of taillights from a 1937 Ford hang on handmade brackets.

While many of us may be able to envision the hot rod of our dreams, Jake is both lucky and talented enough to bring his vision to fruition.

Sectioned and channeled to better fit the truck's contours, the cowling went through extensive modifications.

Bias-ply rubber is stretched over the steel wheels with whitewalls and dog dish hub caps for added flair.

1932 FORD PICKUP "THE WHISKEY"

Owner: JoJo Mialki
Builders: Jojo Mialki and family

Whether he knows it or not, Jojo Mialki is a lucky guy. Not only did he build this hot rod truck at the tender age of 22, but he also had his family's support and assistance in doing so. He had wanted to build such a rod for many years, but his finances curtailed his efforts. This situation changed when he won $10,000 at the craps table to finance his dream. He used his winnings to pay for his dream truck. His family supported his efforts and even pitched in to help him build it. Many of us would consider ourselves fortunate to have any one of those factors in our corner, let alone all of them.

Jojo knew he wanted to build a hot rod for himself one day, and in his head he could almost see the finished product rolling down the roads in Florida, where he lives. What he failed to see were the troubles ahead as the build progressed. Anyone who's ever taken on a task of this nature can tell you of the pitfalls that await, but until you go through it personally, they just don't sink in.

With his gambling winnings in hand, Jojo set out to assemble the truck we see here. Nearly every component and square inch of the truck has been built from scratch, making it a truly "old school" rod. His father, Joe, has been involved in vintage drag racing for many years and his input and knowledge went a long way in building a rod that runs as well as it looks.

Beginning with 2 x 4-inch steel tubing, Jojo welded the chassis into shape, adding the 18-inch "Z" drop at the rear to accommodate the suspension and truck bed. Under the rear frame rails are Model A Ford cross member and leaf springs holding early Ford brake drums in position. The front suspension is composed of a Magnum dropped axle, Ansen friction shocks and a reverse-eye leaf spring. General Motors disc brakes help to haul the truck down from speed. Some 1940 Ford Deluxe steel wheels were painted red before being used at all four corners with the ubiquitous dog-dish wheel covers in place. Firestone bias ply tires with whitewalls are used up front, with a set of Mickey Thompson cheater slicks, also wearing whitewalls, out back.

Power for "The Whiskey" hails from a 1954 Chrysler 331 Hemi mill. Only about 120 copies of these engines were built for NASCAR beach racing in the mid 1950s. Jojo and his dad, Joe, rebuilt the motor to make sure that things were up to par inside before hitting the streets. On the Offenhauser intake manifold you will find a trio of two-barrel Rochester carburetors that draw fuel through a mechanical fuel pump. A matching set of three "mushroom top" air cleaners do their best to keep things clean. It's old school to the highest power!

Fuel storage is the responsibility of the Moon-style tank mounted in the bottomless bed of the truck. Reaching again into the vintage rod handbook, a set of hand-fabricated lake-style exhaust pipes were crafted by Jojo and his family crew. Keeping the retro racing motor cool is a custom built, four-core radiator hidden behind the rat rod cowling. The power is fed to a Turbo 350 gearbox that is featured prominently in the cockpit. A 32-inch-tall shift lever is used to grab the required ratio and looks right at home inside the throwback interior.

He borrowed a set of booth seats from his dad's pizza restaurant and used a blanket purchased at a truck stop for upholstery. His mother helped him fit the blanket over the rectangular, padded cushions. The colorful hues of the blanket are a stark contrast to the diamond plate floor that allows the transmission to breath freely. The steel dashboard is filled with vintage Auto Meter gauges and is decorated with hand painted graphics.

Complementing the dash art are the pin-up girl door panels, also

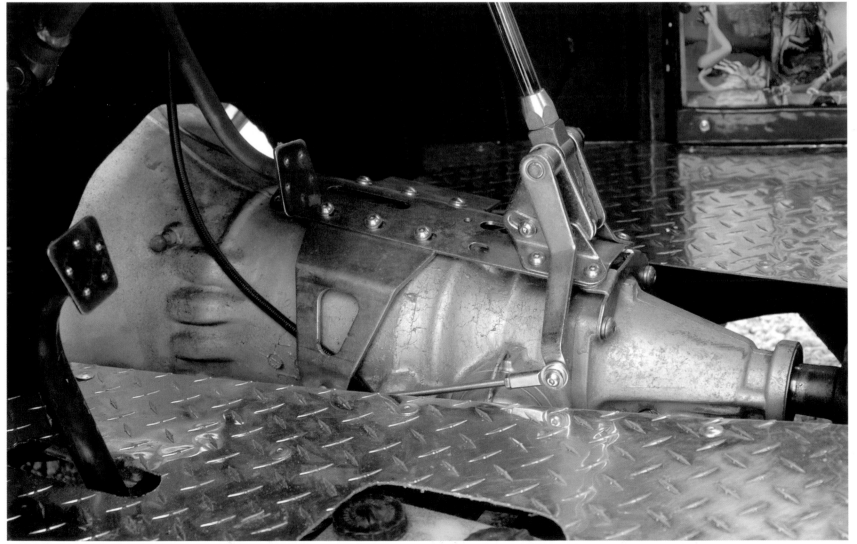

Keeping things simple was the way of the early hot rod builder, and Jojo built his truck using the open transmission mount methods of original rod builders.

"HELL RAISER"

Hand-painted graphics adorn the dashboard of the truck, adding another bit of old school to the assembly.

the work of the owner. A Moon steering wheel has been painted in red metalflake to nicely accent the rest of the confines. The front windshield is a vintage component that tilts out to provide airflow on hot days. The rear opening has been covered with chicken wire to facilitate even better flow. In true hot rod tradition, the truck lacks any form of sound system. With the motor and gearbox sitting in your lap, who could hear a radio anyway?

The steel surrounding the interior is the result of taking the '32 Ford body, chopping out 4-1/2 inches and channeling 5-1/2 inches from the factory dimensions. Any remaining gaps in the metal were filled with steel patch panels and leaded into place.

While the finish may look barn fresh, it is actually a new application of colors to mimic the patina of age. Named "The Whiskey," the truck earned the moniker due to some frustrations during the build process. Jojo's friends claim that more money was spent on alcoholic beverages than on the truck itself, and an empty bottle was used as

the overflow tank up front as a reminder. As we find in many old school rods, the turn signals consist of the driver's arm with bare bones head and taillights. The rear "stop" light was obtained from a 1933 model for use on this '32.

Numerous Old-World touches add to the magic of this modern-day build. The window visor, mounted where it was meant to be, matches the faded paint scheme and goes almost unnoticed. Welded to the radiator cowling is a rusted horseshoe for another throwback to the early days of rodding. Brightly chromed valve covers on the Hemi engine are one of the few hot spots on the truck with the balance wearing the weathered look of age.

Considering Jojo's young age and that this is his first effort at building a hot rod, I'd say his work has been a success. Having good luck on your side doesn't hurt, but it won't make up for a lack of talent, no matter how hard you try.

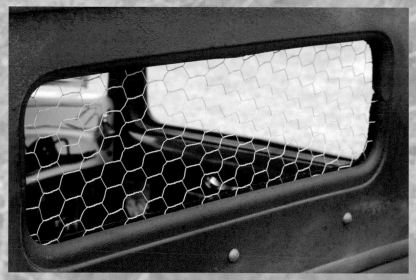

Adding to the free-flow design of the cab, chicken wire was used in lieu of glass in the rear window opening of the truck.

The Moon aluminum fuel tank holds the required fossil fuels in place with style.

The perfect touch to any 1950s rod is the red wheels highlighted by chrome lug nuts and bullet center caps.

1956 FORD F-100

Owner and Builder: Dan Ulreich

When hot rodding was young, people built cars and trucks to meet their own desires, using whatever materials were lying around. High-end shops, rare alloy billets and 24-inch rims were yet to be created, and things were highly individualized. Today's world of hot rods may be more complex, but some owners still adhere to the "rules" of yesteryear when assembling their modern-day vehicles.

Dan Ulreich spends his working days at Midwest Hot Rods, and is himself a talented builder and painter. When deciding to do a truck for himself, he chose the simpler way of life for his creation, but still used nothing but the finest materials to do the job. With a longstanding interest in the 1956 F-100 from Ford, he chose that path to begin his journey.

At first glance the contours of the truck look almost stock, but closer inspection reveals a wide range of modifications to the sheet metal. Beginning with the hood, all emblems were removed and the crest was truncated to meet Dan's plans. Under the all-steel hood we find a firewall with much smoother curves and matching tubs for the front wheels. Although subtle, the alterations are amazing. The satin-black paint that covers every inch of the truck's body has been highlighted with period pinstriping by Bill "Jive" Jarvis, and really makes a nice visual addition to the otherwise dark spread of metal.

Powering the low profile F-100 is a fairly stock 350-cubic-inch engine from Chevrolet. Some mild massaging helps to keep the power delivery smooth and consistent, and appearance mods are abundant. The most obvious is the modern air cleaner that sits atop the four-barrel carburetor.

Using 17 different pieces of aluminum, Dan cut, formed, rolled and welded the segments into one seamless component. The idea had been rolling around in his head for years, and he was excited to finally bring his concept to reality. Work like this separates the professionals from the rest in a hurry. An electric fuel pump sips from the factory storage tank while a set of chrome pulleys glisten within the highly detailed engine compartment. A 700R4 gearbox holds the four speeds in check, and Dan bent a 2-1/2-inch exhaust system for the truck.

Among the many under hood mods, the air cleaner was handmade by Dan himself using 17 different segments of aluminum.

Designed to provide the owner with a measure of protection, this label warns thieves of the consequences of their plans.

Keeping things simple, Dan selected a Chevrolet 350 engine for his Ford and teamed it with a 700R4 automatic transmission.

Nestled in the newly smoothed out dash is the original 1956 speedometer.

What's the sense of looking cool when you can't be cool? This under-dash A/C unit does what it can to keep the occupants comfortable during hot summer days.

The rolled-and-pleated upholstery continues onto the inner door panels for a bright and consistent look.

The satin-black paint that covers the truck is highlighted with perfectly applied striping at all crucial locations.

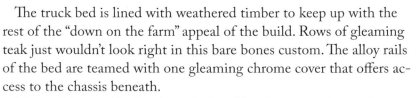

The truck bed is lined with weathered timber to keep up with the rest of the "down on the farm" appeal of the build. Rows of gleaming teak just wouldn't look right in this bare bones custom. The alloy rails of the bed are teamed with one gleaming chrome cover that offers access to the chassis beneath.

Most of the truck's chassis and related hardware remain stock, but as with all true hot rod builders, Dan couldn't leave well enough alone. An independent front suspension was added to the mix for improved handling and a lowered stance. Out back, the factory axle was relocated to the top of the leaf springs for a dropped position to match the new front end dimensions. A pair of 11-inch disc brakes on the front wheels is mated to a set of more basic drums at the rear, but the combination does an adequate job of dropping speeds to legal levels when required. Steel wheels, painted bright red, are finished off with chrome lug nuts and gleaming chrome bullet caps in the centers.

B. F. Goodrich rubber measuring 225/70R-15 in front and 255/70R-15 at the back keeps things quiet and safe. The whitewalls only add to the "old school" charm of the truck.

The spacious cabin of the F-100 has been addressed from all angles, and combines classic rodding with modern technology. Using the factory Ford bench seat and covering it with bright red upholstery brings a new level of zeal to the interior. The rol-and-pleated pattern is repeated on both door panels, which are also lavished in the bright red material. The steel dashboard was relieved of some of the factory edges before being painted and striped to accompany the outside of the truck. A Ford speedometer is joined by a bank of VDO gauges to provide Dan with a full complement of information.

The stock steering wheel has been retained, but the three-on-the-tree shift lever has been altered to allow for gear selections from the automatic transmission now installed. The under-dash air conditioning unit provides cool air during those hot summer nights, and the JVC audio system delivers ample volume whether the windows are up or down. Peering through the factory glass we find the period perfect shrunken head dangling from the rearview mirror. We will safely assume that this is merely a replica and not a previous foe of Dan's.

Outside lighting on the '56 is all Ford, with a pair of cat-eye covers added to the headlamps.

It took Dan a little more than eight months to complete his '56 dream truck, and new revisions are already in the works. As we all know, a true hot rod guy is never satisfied with his current ride, no matter how cool it may be. Methods to make it faster, slicker or more unusual are always being introduced, keeping the project alive until the current or next owner decides otherwise.

1962 DODGE BROTHERS

Owner: Thomas Szymanski
Builder: Thomas Szymanski and friends

We can thank Thomas' two uncles for inspiring him to build this rod. Back in the 1960s, both of his relatives were members of a club called "The Belvideres." Thomas recalled racing their five-window coupe at US 30 as well as other local venues. This exposure to hot rods and racing not only started but also peaked his interest in one day building a rod of his own. It was nearly 40 years later, but Thomas finally got some friends together, and by spending four hours every Monday night they assembled the car we see here. Using the one-day-a-week plan, it took nearly two years to complete the assembly.

Construction began by selecting a 1923 chassis from Total Performance. This modern day chassis uses the vintage dimensions with up-to-date materials for a safe and stable platform. The front I-beam suspension is hung with Ford Maverick rotors that are clamped by General Motors calipers.

Steel rims are capped with Moon discs and P215/70R-14 Firestone rubber keeps things quiet. The rear suspension also hails from a Ford Maverick and a pair of Ford drum brakes provides the anchors. Lurking behind the full coverage Moon disc caps are steel wheels painted half black and half white. This style of painting is true old school hot rod, but is seldom seen on today's iterations. More Firestone rubber, measuring P235/75R-15 on the back rims, provides traction when the loud pedal is pressed into action.

Built Rite was assigned the task of assembling the Chevrolet 305-cubic-inch V-8 engine that powers the car along. An Edelbrock 600 carburetor feeds the fuel to the mill and Chrome Classic T-Bucket four-into-one headers lead the exiting fumes astray.

Mixing brands with modern and vintage steel equates to a well-equipped dashboard in this '26 Dodge Brothers car.

Floor mounted for convenience, the three-speed shift mechanism is trimmed with the requisite skull shift knob.

The annoyance of mufflers has been forgone in true hot rod fashion. The air cleaner was borrowed from a 1950s vintage General Motors car and is adorned with another devilish detail. Chrome pulleys add some flash to the open motor. The build team also chose to apply sections of the same mint green paint to the motor as was used on the body of the car. Taken from a '39 Chevy, the four-core radiator keeps the fluids cool as they course through the engine.

The 305-cubic-inch motor feeds the power to a three-speed THM 350 transmission, and sends it through an 11-inch driveshaft that culminates at a Ford eight-inch rear end. No one can accuse Thomas and his crew of choosing favorites when picking pieces for

A set of taillights from a 1959 Cadillac serve on this new millennium rod, and look great doing so.

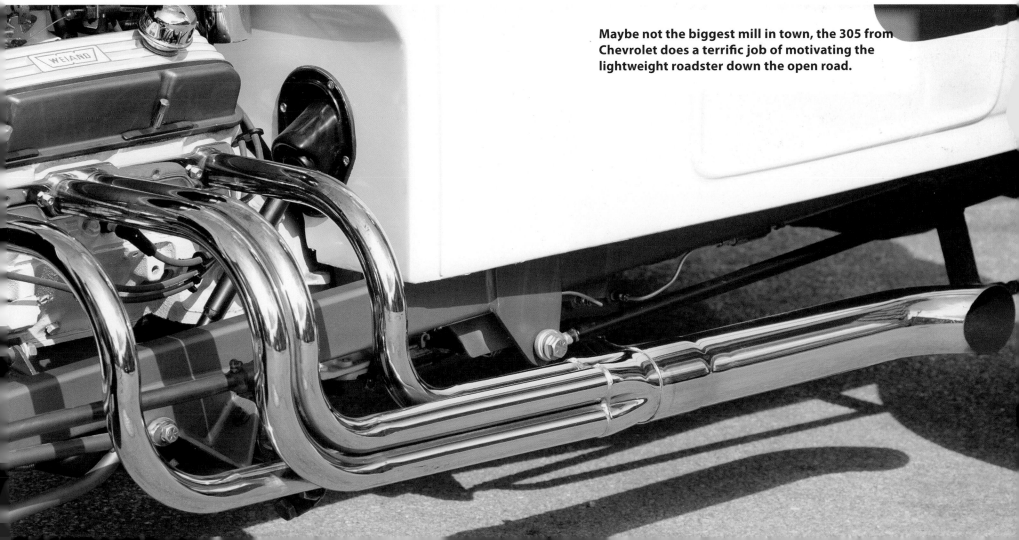

Maybe not the biggest mill in town, the 305 from Chevrolet does a terrific job of motivating the lightweight roadster down the open road.

Perhaps doing duty in a previous life on a Meyer's Manx, the 10-gallon fuel tank was formerly found on a 1960s-era dune buggy.

ILLINOIS · TEMP

250G842

this build. The floor-mounted shift lever is topped off with a tribal décor skull, a perfect addition to this contemporary, old school rod. Ten gallons of fossil fuel can be stored in the cylindrical tank taken from a 1960s era dune buggy.

The assembly of the interior was again achieved by dipping into a variety of parts bins from numerous manufacturers. Seating taken from a Dodge Caravan was bolstered by ABS plastic backing before being upholstered in Ice-White vinyl. As the car sits now, the black, white and gray blanket covers the smooth vinyl seat covers. The dash panel was found in a 1926 Dodge and then fitted with white-faced, Moon-Eye gauges. Modern conveniences include 12-volt outlets for cell phones or other modern devices. The chrome devil face has eyes that light up to indicate turn signal use, as well as braking.

With a steering wheel taken from a Chris-Craft boat, a steering column from a VW Bug, the steering gear from a 1950 Mercury and a steering arm from a model A Ford, we again see that Thomas has no special affiliation with any brand.

Although built with 12-volt accessory outlets, the car lacks a sound system. Driver and passenger gaze through a windshield from a 1927 Ford as they motor down the lane, with no side or rear glass installed.

Mr. Roadster brackets hold the 1962 Dodge headlights in position and a pair of turn signals from the same maker indicates the driver's intentions up front. The taillamps are obviously purloined from a 1959 Cadillac and pull double duty as brake and turn signal lamps. The mint green scallops over the satin black body cast a classic shadow and bring a new level of fun to this home-built hot rod.

1932 FORD ROADSTER

Owner: Jim Talaga
Builders: Everett Gray and Jim Talaga

To some people in the hot rod arena, there's only one car, and that's the 1932 Ford. Whether a coupe, roadster or window body, the hot rodders consider that year and make to be the consummate hot rod of all time. Whether you agree with that outlook or not, you'd have to agree that this two-tone example is one of the nicest around.

The owner had purchased a complete set of Jaguar suspension bits a decade earlier with no real plans of where they would end up. Having built and owned several hot rods in his life, he finally decided to build a high-end '32 that would roll on the Jaguar running gear. Once the path was chosen, it took two years to complete the car. No detail was overlooked, and no expense was spared when designing the body, paint and all of the related trim and hardware.

The payoff for taking that level of time was its use on the official PPG "Outstanding Use of Color" promotional posters, and inclusion on the NSRA's 2005 advertising campaign. Numerous magazine features and "best of show" trophies have also been garnered by this amazing hot rod, so the cost and effort did not go unnoticed.

All of the Jaguar running gear needed a home, so a fully boxed chassis was created as the platform. Tubular cross members add rigidity to the equation, and the 105-inch wheelbase makes for a long and comfortable stance. The leading edge of the chassis holds the

Taken from a Jaguar, the independent front suspension delivers great handling and complex good looks.

Taken from a Chevrolet Camaro, the front brakes include ventilated rotors for competent stopping power.

Chevrolet was chosen for the power plant and a 350-cubic-inch throttle body injection unit was installed under the hood.

Additional Jaguar hardware can be found under the rear of the car, complete with inboard brakes from Wilwood.

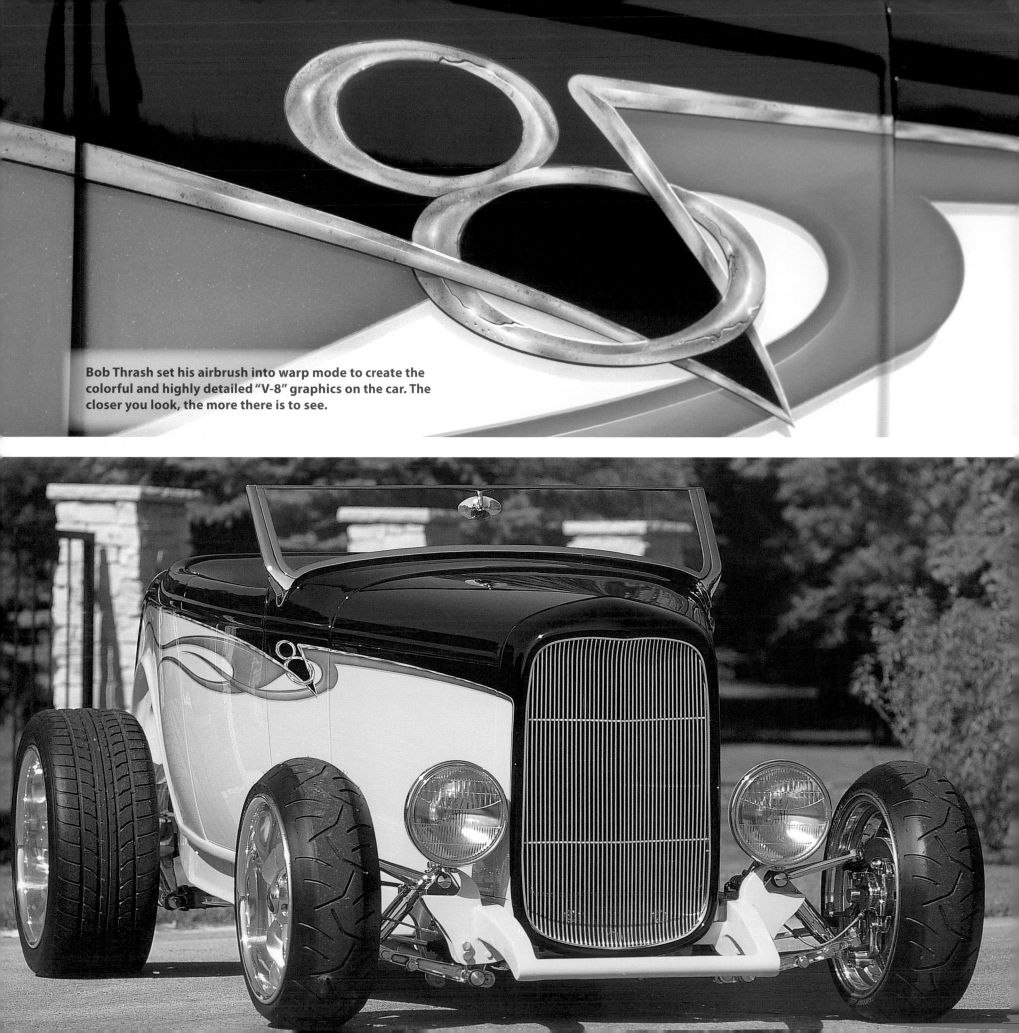

Bob Thrash set his airbrush into warp mode to create the colorful and highly detailed "V-8" graphics on the car. The closer you look, the more there is to see.

With its gently curved top section, the custom-made window frame also required hand-formed glass.

first set of Jaguar independent suspension along with SoCal shocks and Chrysler rack-and-pinion steering.

The front brakes were taken from a Chevrolet Camaro and the large, ventilated rotors do a commendable job of halting forward progress. The brake pressure is moderated by a Corvette master cylinder. A pair of Boyd's 17 x 7-inch "Smoothie" wheels helps to guide the car along and 200-mm motorcycle tires are wrapped around the front hoops. Their round profile not only looks great, but adds a new dimension of low speed handling. The center "V-8" badges are custom made for this car to continue the theme created by the owner.

At the aft end of the frame rails we find a Jaguar independent rear suspension. Wilwood inboard brakes add a touch of race car to the build and look right at home when teamed with the Jag hardware. Positraction and a 3.33 final drive gear deliver terrific performance without breaking a sweat. Another set of "Smoothie" wheels from Boyd hang off the rear axle, complete with their own set of "V-8" center caps. Goodyear 295/40/20 rubber keeps the shiny stuff off the pavement. The retractable license plate slithers up under the

body when the car is parked, providing a clear view of the chrome-plated suspension.

All of this glitter would be nothing without an adequate power plant under the hood, and Jim didn't miss that boat either. A Chevrolet 350 V-8 with throttle port injection was chosen to nestle between the rails. This TPI fuel injection system delivers crisp performance while maintaining a modicum of mileage. Another component is the TPI air cleaner that has been painted to match the exterior Spectrum Yellow hue by PPG. An electric fuel pump keeps the precious fluid flowing without a hitch from the custom-made fuel tank by "Tank."

The tank resides behind the seats of the car for even weight distribution and hide-away good looks. A full length, dual exhaust system was bent from all stainless steel, including the mufflers.

A 700R transmission provides nearly seamless automatic shifting, bringing a new level of comfort to the world of hot rods. Billet Specialties pulleys finish off the engine portion of our tour.

The roadster body features a hood that was custom made by Dan

A pair of gauges from Classic Instruments resides in a dashboard that is also complete with graphics by Bob Thrash.

Both the form and upholstery are handmade for this car by Steve Ralfs and the Garrett Leather was dyed in BlueBerry for this build.

Fink and leads us to the Jim Rench custom grille. Although a subtle feature, the windshield frame is not only canted back by four inches, but carries a gentle curve in its top stretch. The frame was also chopped by 2-1/2 inches to accent the remaining changes. It is details like these that set this rod apart from many others. The custom frame required hand-formed glass to fit, so it was back to the Yellow Pages.

It would be hard to miss the outlandish yellow and blue paint scheme that Jim selected, but that was all a part of his evil plan. The House of Kolor's Kandy Cobalt Blue is perfectly contrasted by the PPG Spectrum Yellow that covers the lower section of the car. The highly detailed dividing graphics are truly a work of art that was produced by Bob Thrash. The closer you look, the more details make themselves known.

The cozy cockpit of the '32 is no less amazing with a bench seat that was made specifically for this car by Steve Ralfs. Once the seating was created, an expanse of Garrett Leather, BlueBerry in color, was stretched over the contours of the form.

Simple perforations in the side panels allow the music from the speakers to flow through and avoid the mess of adding grilles. An Alpine sound system lives within but is hidden from view and allows full control of its many features. A set of gauges from Classic Instruments fills the holes in the dashboard that has also been treated to graphics by Bob Thrash. The "Hollow Point" alloy steering wheel comes from the Billet Specialties catalog and is bound by matching BlueBerry leather.

Although not used here, the car also has a lift-off top that was designed and built by the owner.

It's the small things that make an award-winning rod, and these V-8 wheel centers are but a few of the many touches to be found when exploring this hot '32.

1937 FORD COUPE

Owner/Builder: Jack McKay

Viewing the results of his latest hobby project, a person could easily mistake it for something far more serious. Jack McKay has built other hot rods as a hobby before and admits that it has become more of a passion than a simple pasttime. It beats growing green beans in the backyard, if you ask me. His home shop is as clean and well-equipped as many commercial shops I have seen, and a second project rod is currently in the works. His attention to detail and ability to build to his own exacting demands allows him complete freedom when it comes to creating new cars.

Jack has always liked the lines of the 1937 Ford five-window coupe, and selected it as his latest conquest. Instead of searching the boneyards or Ebay for a donor car, he chose to go the fiberglass route.

After taking delivery of his OZE Rod Shop Fast Back kit, the work began. Even the high quality of this glass body was not enough to satisfy his custom urges, so Jack set out to make the car his own. The fenders were widened, the front grille was shortened and then laid back at a harsher angle and the floor was raised by three inches. Retaining the suicide door configuration, he also added six inches in length to the portals. Being a do-it-himself kind of guy, Jack even sprayed the revised body with the PPG Pearl Orange paint. Additional stripe details, including the gold leaf inserts, were another touch of his design, talent. Once inside the coupe we find a tastefully appointed cockpit. A set of Pontiac Fiero Recaro-edition seats were covered in the beige leather by Schober's Upholstery. The wraparound dash holds VDO gauges in place to monitor the car's basic functions at all times. The sweeping center console was hand formed and carries the HVAC and radio controls as well as several small rocker switches for

The VDO gauges are clustered in this elliptical alloy housing, making for a clean presentation.

The wraparound dash, flowing center console and luxury appointments all add up to concours-quality cockpit.

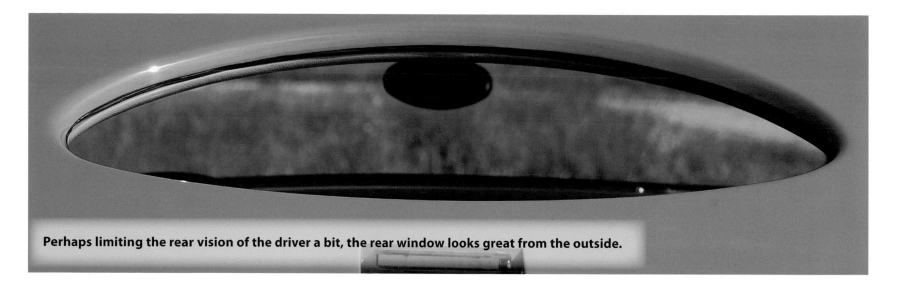

Perhaps limiting the rear vision of the driver a bit, the rear window looks great from the outside.

After being stolen from a Recaro edition Fiero, the seats were then upholstered in beige leather to compliment the rest of the luxurious cockpit.

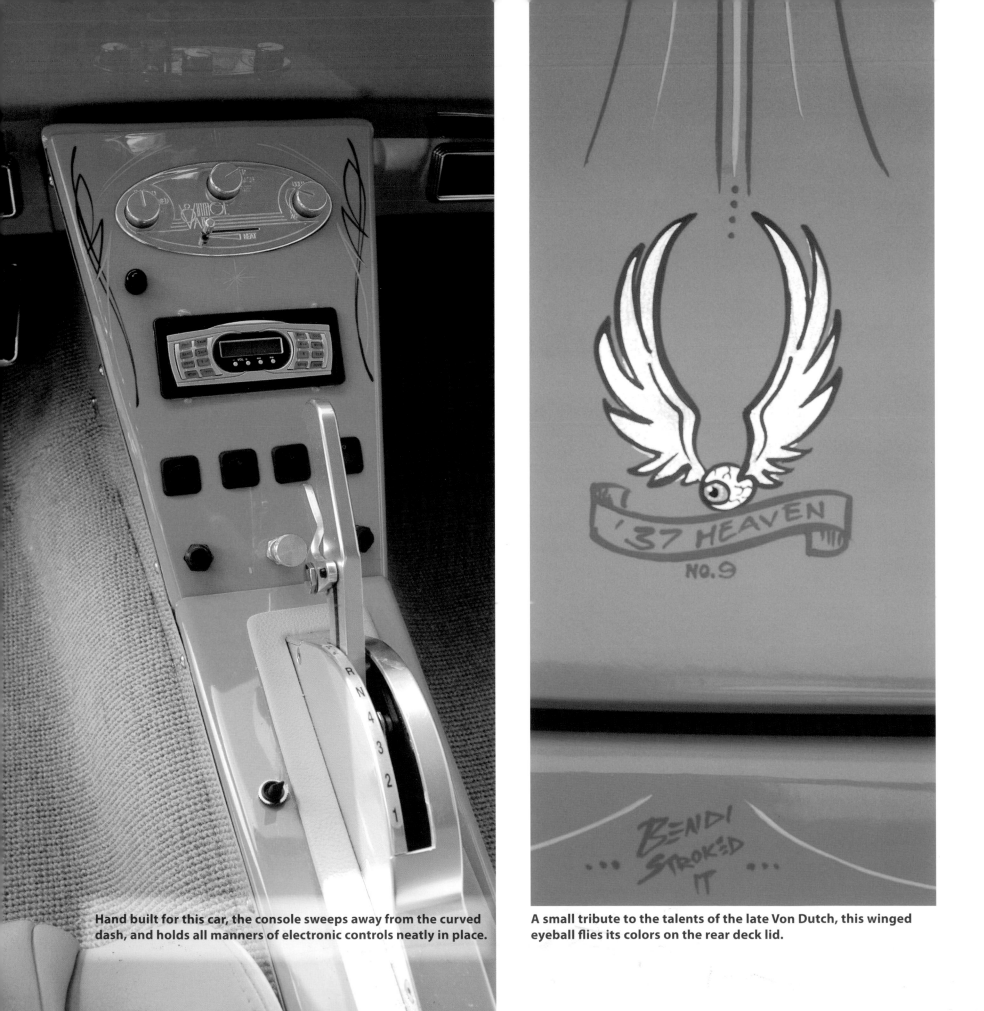

Hand built for this car, the console sweeps away from the curved dash, and holds all manners of electronic controls neatly in place.

A small tribute to the talents of the late Von Dutch, this winged eyeball flies its colors on the rear deck lid.

lights and related electronic goodies. The polished alloy shift lever is also found here and is perfectly matched to the other metal bits found inside the car. Inside panels of matching materials offset the still-visible Pearl Orange on each door. A Billet Specialties steering wheel is also wrapped with matching beige leather to complete the ensemble.

OZE Rod Shop was also tapped for the chassis under the '37's bodywork. The front suspension comes in the form of the popular Mustang II hardware, complete with coil-over springs. The General Motors brake discs measure 11 inches in diameter up front, and can be viewed easily through the open face of the Billet Specialties 17-

inch rims. Goodyear tires keep the dazzling wheels from the pavement, if only by the slimmest of sidewalls.

A four-link rear suspension carries a Ford eight-inch rear end with another set of coil-over springs for comfort and control. Another pair of GM 11-inch brakes can also be seen through the 20-inch wheels hanging off the rear axle. The Goodyear rubber supply was depleted by two with the addition of their massive rear meats.

Hoping for the "all show, no go" routine, Jack mounted a 350-cu-bic-inch Chevrolet small block V-8 into the engine bay. The engine is another of Jack's accomplishments, with the assembly credited to him alone.

A traditional 350-cubic-inch mill from Chevrolet powers this 1937 coupe.

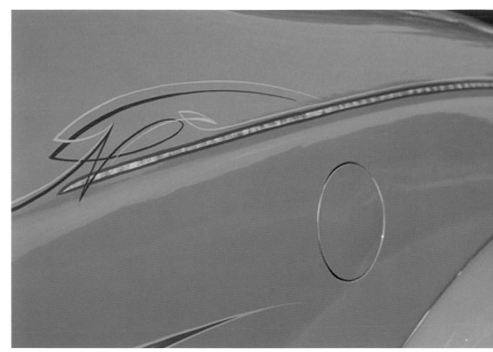

The PPG Pearl Orange paint is highlighted by pinstripes and gold leaf accents.

The choice of the 600-cfm carburetor was made to deliver adequate fuel while retaining the desired rumble at idle.

A single Edelbrock 600-cfm carburetor feeds the fuel and air mix to the motor, and Jack chose this method over the more modern fuel injection on purpose. While the fuel injection system delivers seamless acceleration at any rpm, it doesn't rumble at idle like a carburetor does, hence his decision to go with a carb.

The Billet Specialties catalog was again used to purchase the alloy air cleaner mounted astride the lone carburetor. Fuel storage is handled by a Tank's unit. Flowmaster 50 Series mufflers handle the noise suppression and are only a portion of the stainless exhaust system that runs beneath the chassis of the '37. An AFCO aluminum radiator keeps the vital fluids cool, while a 700R4 transmission delivers automatic gear selection.

Working in his home shop/garage, it took Jack 18 months to complete this build. Judging by the slickness of the final ride, I'd have guessed it took much longer to build this car. Yet, when passion is in your corner, almost anything can happen.

The height and stance of the grille were altered to achieve this more aggressive lean angle.

1937 Ford Coupe ~ **65**

1932 FORD ROADSTER

Owner/Builder: Steve Metz

Steve Metz has built and driven a number of hot rods in his days, but decided to build one that was both fast and comfortable. In addition to making the car look terrific, he wanted all the creature comforts of a family sedan. Besides massive horsepower, he demanded air conditioning and working heat, a great sound system and as a roof that would keep him dry in inclement weather. It took more than seven years, but this amazing roadster is the fruit of his labors.

The project is built around a pinched frame from Barry Cobecks. This platform provided Steve with the stiffness and features he needed for his functioning hot rod. A Pete & Jakes four-bar rear end is suspended by coil-over shocks, and the entire assembly has been polished to a mirror-like finish. Wilwood disc brakes are hidden behind a pair of Colorado Custom 20-inch rims with Dunlop rubber providing traction. For control up front, a four-inch dropped axle was installed, again with coil-over shocks taking the bumps out of the ride. Another set of Wilwood rotors and calipers were polished to a gleam, and also provided plenty of slowing power. Colorado Custom 18-inch rims are mounted to the front axle with a matching set of Dunlop donuts for grip.

Slipping a motor from a 1972 Chevy Suburban, the 454-cubic-inch mill was then massaged to life by Step-Up Performance. Cylinder dimensions now measure .30 over factory specs for an added push when the need arises.

The big block monster is fed through two Edelbrock 600-cfm carburetors, each a four-barrel model. A mechanical fuel pump from Holley pulls fuel from the tank to the carbs through braided stainless lines. Fuel economy was not a factor when building the car and only a 15-gallon fuel tank behind the seats

Wanting as much "show" as he did "go," Steve installed a 454-cubic-inch mill between the front rails of his '32 chassis.

holds the precious fluid in place. A Billet Specialties air cleaner sits atop the pair of Edelbrocks to keep stray animals from being pulled into the vortex. A set of polished pulleys from Zoops and chrome valve covers bearing the words "Yabba Dabba Do" help dress up the business-like engine bay. An aluminum radiator keeps the system in the right temperature range and looks good while doing it.

A 700R4 gearbox sends the requested horsepower to the 3.50 rear end, complete with Positraction via a polished driveshaft. We are beginning to see why it took seven years to complete the car, since almost every item not painted has been highly polished.

In his efforts to build a comfortable, yet fast street rod, Steve chose a custom bench seat, then covered the gentle contours with ultra leather for looks and longevity. Since he spent seven years building the beast, he has no immediate plans to get rid of it.

When the roof has been brought along, but isn't required, it stows neatly behind the seat, ready for action in the event of rain.

Polished to a soft glow, the exhaust headers do their twisted best to make a clear path for the rapidly exiting gases. A 2-1/2-inch dual exhaust system beneath the roadster shows them the way.

Sporting a set of reversed and flipped Honda taillights, the rear deck of the '32 is finished with a one-of-a-kind license plate frame that was built for this car specifically.

A custom-produced alloy panel holds the Auto Meter gauges neatly in place and adds another touch of "hand-built" to this creation.

A Billet Specialties steering wheel has been coddled in the same ultra leather as the seats to conform to the consistent nature of the build.

Not only is the cockpit simple and elegant, but it also boasts air conditioning, heat and a full range of audio options.

While the set of Auto Meter Phantom gauges would have looked great poking out through the standard steel dash of the '32, Steve went the extra mile and had a one-of-a-kind aluminum dash panel crafted. This swooping bit of alloy holds the instruments in place with style. Another ellipse of alloy, complete with a ribbed surface, holds the Chrysler AM/FM/CD/cassette unit in position, right in front of where the wire-form cup holders do the same for beverages while tooling down the road.

Of course no hot rod, regardless of power and convenience, can be considered real until wrapped in some sort of body.

The '32 hi-boy convertible here features lengthened doors, a three-inch channel at the front and a hood that has been stretched by six inches.

A custom grille was produced by Jim Rench to complement the sleek lines of the roadster's form. Layers of DuPont's Smooth Yellow paint were applied and lovingly rubbed into submission to achieve the seamless finish. A set of sealed-beam headlights from Dietz light the way at night, while a pair of taillights taken from a Honda were used out back. Before being integrated into the body they were reversed left to right and flipped 180 degrees from what the factory had in mind.

Nestled between the Honda lights is a license frame that again was designed and crafted for this car specifically. Carved from a block of billet aluminum, the frame makes a real statement on a car that already makes itself known.

Not only was Steve not in a rush to finish the car, he wasn't willing to use any old factory bolt-ons in the process. No step has been avoided and no corners were cut to build this fast and comfortable '32.

At the end of a hood that has been extended by six inches we find a custom grille formed by Jim Rench.

Upholstered in soft and supple ultra leather, the cockpit is more comfortable than many living rooms.

1940 WILLYS

Owner/Builder: Len Meehan

Len has been around hot rods for most of his life, and still has fond memories of the straight-axle gasser cars that ran on the strip in the 1960s. Even then, he thought they were cool and hoped to one day have his own. Maybe it was a self-fulfilling prophecy, but after watching cars strafe the quarter mile for years, Len got into owning his own hot rods. This 1940 Willys is not his first hot rod, but has been in his garage for 16 years. Others will follow, but his efforts with this classic vehicle go on without hesitation.

Unlike many of the fiberglass-bodied cars we see these days, Len's car is a true steel-bodied Willys. Wanting to keep the car as close to his memories as possible, absolutely no modifications have been made to the shell of this prewar beauty.

The vivid Chrysler Intense Blue paint isn't stock, but suits the curvaceous body of the Willys to a T. In stark contrast to the unaltered body of the car, everything else inside and underneath has been modified for racing applications.

Hoisting the steel hood reveals a Chrysler 354-cubic-inch Hemi V-8 dating back to 1956. With racing in mind, Len had the engine built by Motion Dynamics for that purpose. Bolted atop the blue-printed mill is a 671 blower for added boost at the track, or on the street. Delivering fuel to the hungry cylinders is a Hilborn four-port electronic fuel injection system. Two fuel tanks are installed, one carrying only two gallons of race-quality petrol while 10 gallons of street-legal juice are held in the other. Making way for the spent fumes are S&S fenderwell headers leading directly to Flowmaster mufflers that are built with a

The one-piece front windshield is original Willys and only a single wiper has the responsibility of wiping the rain away.

The 354-cubic-inch Chrysler Hemi is paired with a 671 blower for added boost and reduced times at the drag strip.

Nothing says old school like a straight axle up front. The tubular dropped axle holds the front wheels in place and the nose of car high.

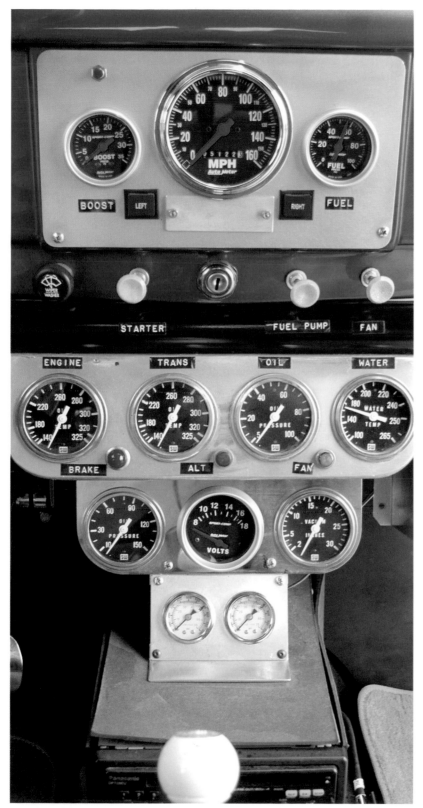

With enough instrumentation to land a small aircraft, Len is never left to wonder about any function of the car and its motor.

Other hints at the car's heritage are the factory badges seen on the car, this one is sandwiched between the trunk handle and license plate illumination.

three-inch opening at either end. By removing the cut-out plates on the headers, a much more direct route can be found for the exhaust. With this truncated exit comes a much higher noise level, so that option is used only at the track.

Cooling the race motor are Chevrolet big block tanks with three-inch copper fins. A dyno run after the motor was complete punched out numbers that read 480 horsepower at 5000 rpm, with 500 foot-pounds of torque. Nothing says "racing engine" like such numbers. The rarity and increasing value of the steel-bodied car limit Len's aggression at the track, but he has still managed to rack up a 12.20-second quarter mile at 111 mph. Not bad for a 66-year-old car weighing in at nearly two tons. Four speeds are available and are chosen through a 700R4 transmission. Driving the rear wheels is a Chevrolet 12-bolt rear end with 4.10 gearing.

One wouldn't expect to find a factory chassis beneath all that power and, in this case, the stock frame rails have been fully boxed for stiffness. Built in true gasser style, the front axle is a tubular dropped version that hangs below a set of Willys leaf springs. The old school of thought put the nose of the car high in the air as a way to put more weight on the drive wheels. Of course, we have since learned that the aerodynamic drag caused by the high-lift front end causes way more resistance to the wind than hoped. Modern day drag machines have their snouts as close to the ground as possible, cutting a cleaner path through the quarter mile of air. Rear suspension duties are handled by factory Willys nine-leaf springs mated to track bars for added control.

Weld RodLite wheels are bolted on at all four corners with Kelly 165R-15 rubber up front and Mickey Thompson 29 x 12.50 donuts on the rear. Lurking behind the classic five-opening rims are Speedway disc brakes on the front with factory Chevrolet drums on the rear.

The cabin of the Willys is sparse, but is decked out with a complete set of instruments for racing use. A simple set of Pontiac Fiero bucket seats are covered in gray "Pleather" with the upholstery done by Moodys. I have seen fewer gauges inside a private plane than what Len has mounted inside the cockpit, but each serves its own function. With all the electronic trickery inside, there was no room left for an audio system, and the music from the Chrysler Hemi is enough for any enthusiast's ears.

Len has no plans to trade this car in for anything else and considers it a work in progress. His ultra-slick garage at home already has another car in the works, and I'll be anxious to see what he turns out next.

A massive pair of Mickey Thompson donuts does their best to get traction when Len puts the squeeze on the loud pedal.

1934 FORD PICKUP

Owner: Jim Talaga
Builder: Jim Talaga and Ken Juricic

With a garage full of gleaming hot rods and classic American cars, Jim decided to build something a bit different when be began this truck. The array of glamorous paints available today is enough to bend your imagination, but Jim wanted his latest hot rod to look as if it had spent the last 50 years behind the barn. Not your typical approach, perhaps, but who's to say it's wrong?

The project began with a 1934 Ford ½-ton pickup. Shortening the stock bed length by 10 inches gave the truck a more aggressive stance. The rear fenders were widened by 1-1/4 inches to make room for the larger-than-stock tires and wheels. The front fenders also gained some girth to allow for the addition of the side-mount spare tire. The front bumper was borrowed from a 1934 automobile in keeping with the random parts selection of a true hot rod.

Obviously, the paint on this car was not something found behind the barn, but carefully applied to mimic the effect. To achieve this multi-colored patina, the entire body was first covered with hot rod black primer. On top of that Jim sprayed or brushed on various hues of Oldsmobile paint to further the results. Final touches of rust were then airbrushed into place strategically to achieve the "barn fresh" look. Although the resulting finish looks rough to the eye, it is as smooth as glass to the touch.

Beneath the prematurely aged sheet metal rolls a 1934 automotive chassis that was boxed in where required for added strength. Front suspension is a collaboration of many parts including a Magnum four-inch dropped axle with a four-bar Panhard. A reversed eye spring meets with a Chevy Vega steering box and '37 Ford spindles.

Wire wheels from a 1953 Cadillac were painted red before being installed under each of the fenders. Behind the front wires we find disc brakes from a 1972 General Motors parts catalog, while the rear anchors are 1992 GMC drum units. The rear tires have grown to a modern, and very healthy 235R75/15 dimension with front

With an aged patina on the paint and red bars in the opening, this modern day truck screams old school.

A truck engine stolen from a 1953 Ford was used as the base for this performance buildup. Polished and painted Offenhauser components boost power and add immensely to the appearance.

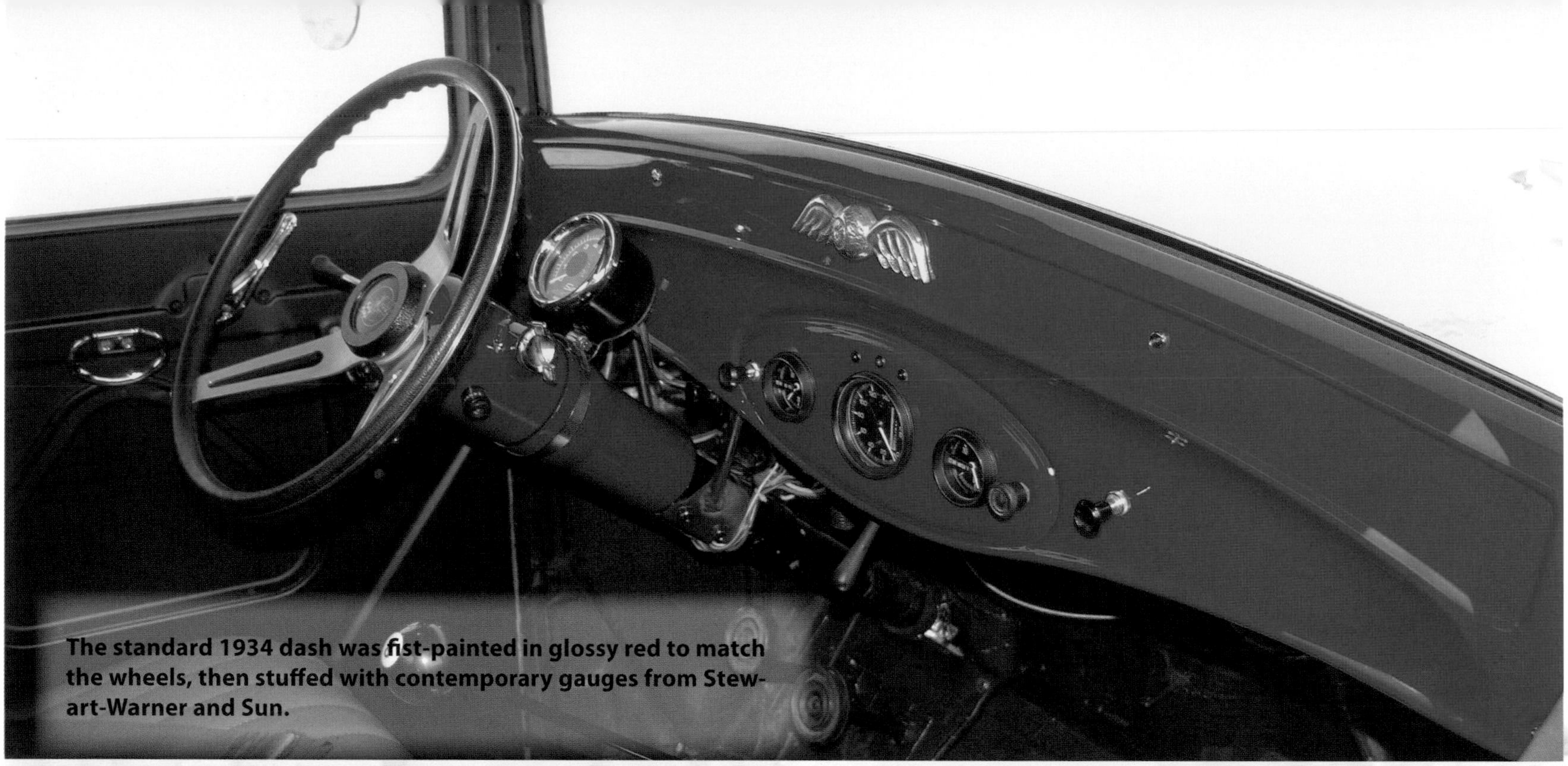

The standard 1934 dash was fist-painted in glossy red to match the wheels, then stuffed with contemporary gauges from Stewart-Warner and Sun.

Shortened by 10 inches before being installed, the bed is lined with finished hardwood and polished alloy trim for a touch of luster to the otherwise aged truck.

TALAGA & SONS

HOT ROD GARAGE

Plainfield, IL.

Est. 1956

With a performance-enhanced engine residing within, the hood's louvers help to keep things cool. Not your usual location for a spare tire, Jim decided the space made a great spot even though the fenders had to be widened for such use.

rubber measuring 165R75/15. She may look old and decrepit, but modern rubber keeps things safe.

Hidden behind the louvered hood we find a motor that began life in a 1953 Ford truck. Displacing 239 cubic inches, the engine was rebuilt to modern day specs by Jim and his pal, Ken Juricic. Heads and an intake from Offenhauser were polished and painted before adding the triple-carb setup. Three individual Moon air cleaners look right at home and do a fair job of keeping small animals from being pulled in.

A Holley electric fuel pump ensures adequate fuel delivery from the 1934 Ford fuel tank that was modified to fit into the truck's frame. A set of Speedway headers was modified for use, then jet-coated for heat resistance. The fumes flow through these headers into a handmade stainless steel exhaust system complete with cutouts. Stainless Speedway mufflers reduce the noise as long as the cutouts aren't in use, and then it's anyone's game. The pulleys and radiator are altered slightly from stock, while a 1948 Ford truck gearbox is employed for changing gears. The open-drive design carries three-speeds in its top-loader configuration and sends power to the rear wheels through an exposed driveshaft.

The cabin of this brand new, barn-fresh truck is nicely done with custom-made seating covered in red "pleather" for plenty of comfort on long journeys. The original 1934 dashboard was painted the same red as the wheels and is fitted with Stewart-Warner gauges and a Sun tachometer. A General Motors tilt steering wheel provides an added touch of comfort and the steering wheel from a Corvair falls neatly into the driver's hands. An auxiliary heating unit by Vintage Air keeps the cabin cozy, even in the coldest of conditions. No sound system, save the melody from under the hood, can be heard no matter how hard you try. Brand new safety glass was used to enclose the truck's inhabitants with clarity and security.

Exterior lighting is simple and in keeping with the flavor of the build. The factory headlight bar was trimmed by two inches and carries period headlights adapted for modern bulbs. Some 1937 Ford taillights were revised for use out back, and each of the four lamps carries custom built-in turn signals to keep things clean. Then again, with a truck designed not to look clean, how tidy should we get?

While attending a recent hot rod event, Jim was approached by none other than legendary builder, Boyd Coddington. Boyd had his eyes and his checkbook ready to buy the truck from Jim, but having just completed the project, Jim was in no mood to sell. To build a vehicle that draws the attentions of one of the country's top builders is saying something, especially in today's world of high-end hot rods.

SLOPPY JALOPY

Owner: George Mostardini
Builders: George Mostardini,
Brian Helmintoler/Felony Chops 'N' Rodz

Although the reasons may be different, there comes a time in every hot rodder's life when the decision is made to build a car. It may not be the first, and probably won't be the last, but still something new must be created.

After spending time at a local car show with friends, George suddenly came to the conclusion that he needed to build a new rod. Talk of an upcoming event only 30 days away sent his mind reeling as he started to put the ball into play. Before the day was over, he could see his next creation in his mind, and knew that less than 30 days from now he'd have to be behind the wheel. Of course his friends thought him crazy, but what are friends for?

His first thoughts were to simply chop an existing model to come up with something drivable, but that didn't seem too original, and George has a penchant for being a little off-center. The nature of a true hot rod builder is to create cars that are rare and unusual, and with this in mind George chose to build a car from scratch. Keep in mind his deadline for completion was only 30 days away, and he held a full-time job as well. George set his sights on driving his latest rod to the big show. Some guys just need their feet held to the fire to perform at their peak.

Maybe he is some sort of visionary, but he had purchased a 1989 Chevrolet Caprice station wagon a few months back, just in case this sort of thing came up. His friend, Brian, had just completed his own rat rod, and as always had some spare parts from donor cars littering his shop. With some of the major components at his avail, he realized George still had lots of little stuff to find and do.

First and foremost was his lack of a chassis. Not letting a trifle like this slow him down, a trip to the steel store

Rising eight inches in the front and 19 inches in the rear, the frame rails take extreme bends to meet with the rest of the car's hardware.

The Oldsmobile 307-cubic-inch V-8 fits snugly between the 8-inch rise in the frame rails and delivers ample power to the 2,130 lb. car.

Equally sparse is the cockpit of the Sloppy Jalopy with only the barest of necessities being employed.

satisfied his needs for the 2 x 4-inch tubing required to weld up the frame. Keeping his radical approach in mind, the rails are angled up at eight inches in the front and 19 inches at the rear. These dynamics would provide him with the cradle he needed to hang the remaining bits and pieces in fitting style.

Slung between the front rails, we find an Oldsmobile 307-cubic-inch engine with a single Holley 650-cfm carburetor. The secondaries and choke are manual, in keeping with the traditional ways of hot rod builders.

Six stubby two-inch diameter exhaust pipes lead the spent fumes away from the engine with no additional muffling to be seen. A radiator taken from a 1965 Ford Mustang is joined with an electric fan to boost the cooling capabilities. An automatic 200R transmis-sion sends the power to the 1978 Impala rear end.

The rear Model A mono-leaf suspension was taken from the remains of Brian's 1929 donor car and modified to work with the modern axle. The rear brakes are the only ones you'll find on this rod, and they too are from the '78 Impala. The front suspension also hails from the same 1929 Ford and is reversed and hung in true suicide fashion.

A set of tall, 21-inch front wheels is of the same 1929 vintage and covered in Firestone rubber. The rear hoops are Titan Racing Equipment hardware and measure 15 x 8 inches with Coker Classic tires delivering the needed traction. In between the rear wheels, we find a pair of recycled compressed oxygen tanks that now hold 4-1/2 gallons of fuel each.

A 1929 Model A Ford split-wishbone front axle was flipped around and mounted in suicide style in keeping with tradition.

First used as compressed oxygen tanks, the gas tanks now hold 4-1/2 gallons of fuel apiece and are the only storage on board.

495 798
ILLINOIS 1940

VOODOO KINGS

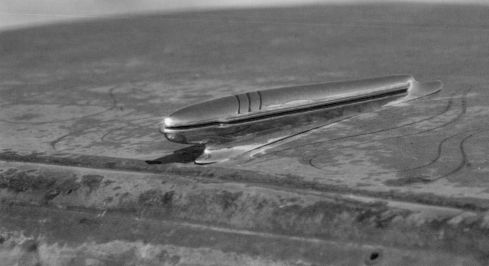

The only shiny bit on the entire car is this Chevrolet hood ornament taken from the 1950s.

George's friend Bob found the body for the project near the Wisconsin border, although when the body was discovered it lacked doors. The guy that sold them the body was able to put them together with another gentleman who sold them the proper pieces. Once home with their newfound steel, the pieces fit together as if made for each other. George had the doors properly fitted, and cut six inches out of the height in a single evening session. The resulting bodywork retains its original patina of age, but has been garnished with some tasteful pinstriping. The black lines will be the only paint the car ever receives.

Inside the car, we find similar trappings when it comes to comfort and convenience. The driver's seat is taken from a vintage farm tractor, and George made the passenger pillion in response to his girlfriend's complaints about riding on a beer cooler. Folded south of the border blankets provide the only upholstery in use.

Lacking any of the original gauges, the dashboard has a small panel welded in place that holds the two SunPro® instruments to monitor temperature, volts and oil pressure. Speed and rpm are seat-of-the-pants guesses at best. The 15-inch diameter steering wheel is wrapped in the finest grade of black electrician's tape available and fits the motif perfectly. Gate locks are installed to hold the doors closed, and seem to do the job well enough. The body lacks any glass and makes for some nice wind-in-the-hair motoring.

Another farm tractor gave its headlights for the project, and appropriate devil taillight lenses were installed for the final touch. The only bit of glamour comes in the form of a 1950s Chevrolet hood ornament mounted to the roof of the car.

It seemed like a crazy and impossible task, but George was able to create and assemble this car in his own garage in the 30-day time period allotted. He and Brian have since created a shop to build similar cars for outside clients, and it'll be interesting to see what rolls out of their doors next.

1929 FORD/1946 DODGE

Owner/Builder: Brian Helmintoler

Brian is often queried as to why he built a car that looks like this, and his answer is always the same: "If you have to ask, you wouldn't understand."

While this same response is popular among those who ride Milwaukee-built motorcycles, the train of thought is the same. There are those who take a different path in life and who find that the usual vehicles simply don't fill their needs to be true individuals.

When Brian found this project car, it had been resting in a garage for 17 years and had become so stacked with clutter that it was difficult to see. The former owner and his grandson had planned on doing the car themselves, but finally gave up their ambitions and sold it to Brian. Once pulled free of the storage space, it was listed as a true basket case with parts in a number of containers there was no road map or instruction sheet to be found. It would take Brian four months to bring it all together.

Once home in his garage, the 1929 Ford Model A Tudor body was chopped by seven inches and shortened by two feet to achieve the look Brian desired. A pickup bed from a 1946 Dodge was truncated by five feet and narrowed 14 inches to match the profile of the body. Once modified it was reconnected using copper rivets for appearance and strength. Welding the seams would have worked equally well, but would not have looked as cool. The original vinyl roof material was removed, leaving the wooden factory spars exposed, as well as Brian and any passenger that rides along.

The open-roof design of his car made his interior decision simple. Nothing inside could be too sensitive to rain or other inclement conditions. To meet Brian's parameters, aluminum racing seats from Kirkey were installed for pilot and co-pilot. The 1929 dashboard is devoid of any gauges, but a cluster of Sun instruments has been relocated below the dash on the frame of the door. The home-built exhaust is the only sound system on board, continuing the no-frills theme of the cockpit. The steering wheel is straight off of a 1929 Model A with no frills or upgrades to its barren surfaces. A glass windshield was installed,

Bolted to the floor in their unadulterated aluminum form, the racing seats don't say much in the way of comfort, but look just fine.

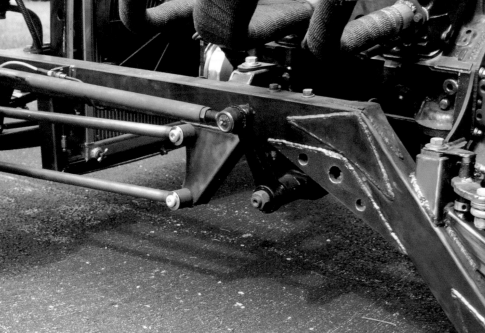

Constructed from 2 x 3-inch steel tubing, the front section of the rails carry a "Z" measuring 13 inches up front.

Another bit of home-made fun can be seen in the trio of velocity stacks that stick up vertically from the Rochester carbs.

but no other panes of protection can be seen. This makes it handy to use the turn signals, which involves motioning with ones left arm.

Scoffing at the mere mention of paint, the car's body remains in a bare metal finish. Caring for this sort of skin requires an occasional oil rubdown to protect it from excessive rust, although a little oil only adds to the mystique. A few bits of pinstriping and graphic art have been added to break up the monotony of the metal.

The raw metal bodywork is carried by a handmade frame crafted from 2 x 3-inch steel tubing. A 13-inch "Z" was added to the front rails and a 24-1/2-inch lift was used in the rear. The four-inch dropped axle up front is mounted in suicide style and is joined by

a Chevrolet Vega steering box. Brian chose to add disc brakes to the front end of his car. While he is often mocked for his decision, he prefers confident stopping to match his aggressive acceleration. A 10-bolt rear end came from a 1979 Camaro and was mated to a fully-adjustable four-link suspension that Brian designed. NAS-CAR-inspired wedge bolts allow the car's height to be adjusted with the turn of a screw.

The rear brakes are from 1929 Ford and do little to slow the car on their own. Vintage Gennie wheels are mounted at all points, with 15 x 5-inch wheels used on the leading edge and 15 x 8-inch wheels bringing up the rear.

Hung in true suicide fashion, the front axle dangles precariously from the heavy-duty bracket.

With a body that was chopped
seven inches, the rear window
opening is obviously a bit lower
than in its previous configuration.

DODGE

449-547

VOODOO KINGS
NO.ILLINOIS

A pair of Firestone cheater slicks was mounted to the rear rims for a real touch of nostalgia. Only the thinnest of grooves in their otherwise flat surface keeps them legal on the streets.

Retaining the factory 1929 grille shell brings another hint of vintage to the overall build, but behind it lies some fairly modern hardware. A custom-built aluminum radiator can be found tucked behind the '29 shell and another bit of homemade gear can be seen in the stone guard.

The reason for the modern cooling arrangement is the chosen power plant was borrowed from a 1991 Chevrolet. The 350 mill is still in bone-stock configuration and was purchased on the word of the owner that it ran before dragging it home. While the block of the motor remains factory, a number of hot rod tricks have been employed to complete the assembly. An Offenhauser intake and a trio of Rochester carburetors deliver the desired mix of fuel and air while the velocity stacks are of Brian's creation. In lieu of the mechanical fuel pump, Brian added a Holley electric unit with a regulator to bring fluid from the 10-gallon, spun aluminum storage tank.

Since building this car, Brian and George have opened their own hot rod shop named Felony Chops 'N' Rodz. They plan on building similar cars for clients who yearn for something different, and with no two creations even close to being alike, we suspect they'll be very busy soon.

A set of Firestone cheater slicks provides all the traction Brian needs, regardless of how heavy his application of the accelerator may be.

1937 FORD CABRIOLET "SHAZAM"

Owner: Jim Talaga
Builders: Jim Talaga and Ken Juricic

There are some hot rod projects that roll down the highway only weeks or months after being imagined. Others are longer term prospects that sit and germinate until work begins. Jim Talaga bought this 1937 Ford 20 years ago, but did nothing with it until recently. He had always liked the body style and knew that one day he'd create a hot rod, but life's chores and work kept him from doing so sooner. While the car sat in silence, Jim was formulating his plan of action regarding the power plant, color scheme and all the other details needed to build his perfect rod.

One of his priorities was to drive a hot rod powered by a big block motor. He could appreciate the nostalgic angle of a flathead mill, but wanted thundering horsepower at his command instead. Along with the big lump under the hood, he wanted the colors to be something different. In a world that is so full of options, this would seem to be a simple task. To achieve the mix of hues we see on this car, Jim blended, sprayed and sampled until he hit the nail on the head. Then, and only then, did he lay down the colors on the sleek body.

Once the decision was made to begin construction, Jim turned to The Roadster Shop in Elgin, Illinois for the chassis. Their reputation for delivering perfectly crafted, turn-key frames made the decision an easy one. The front suspension is a mix of Ford Mustang, Heidt's and Shock Wave air ride hardware. Stopping power comes through a set of Wilwood discs and calipers that are well hidden behind the Billet Specialties 17 x 7-inch alloy rims. Yokohama tires keep things rolling smooth and quiet. A nine-inch Ford rear end complete with traction lock and a set of 3.55 gears takes its orders from the 350 turbo racing gearbox that hangs off the back of the motor. Another set of Billet Specialty wheels, these measuring 20 x

The split-glass windshield harkens back to the early days of automobile design and looks right at home on this modern-day custom.

Looking every bit the vintage gauges they mimic, the Classic instruments deliver modern accuracy.

MPH

Electric Adjustable

0 0 0 2 5 3 4

Classic Instruments

Wanting a dashboard that wrapped around him, Jim designed it to do so and then lead into the graceful lines of the custom door panels.

Matching winged logos were used on both the upper seating surfaces and the alloy boot. Covering the roof when it's hidden away is a hand-formed aluminum boot that fits neatly into the truck when not in use.

The subtle contours of the molded door panels also carry the ductwork for the air conditioning in stealthy style.

8-1/2 inches, are hung on the aft with Yokohama donuts providing traction.

Now that we know how it rolls, let's examine what makes the car go. Jim's desire to use a big-block mill was not ignored and a Chevrolet 454 was used as the host for a raft of upgrades. Competition-grade camshafts and lifters ensure that things stay together regardless of what is asked of them. A matching set of Edelbrock four-barrel carburetors feeds the eager mill, after receiving the fuel via the Holley electric fuel pump. The precious liquid is drawn from a 20-gallon reserve crafted by Ken Juricic.

The artfully shaped, aluminum air cleaner is another product of Ken's skilled hands, as is the 2-1/2-inch stainless steel exhaust. Store-bought mufflers are also done in stainless steel to provide a maximum life expectancy with just the right amount of sound suppression. Billet Specialties pulleys add another bit of flair under the hood and a Walker radiator keeps things cool.

With 20 years to plan the build, Jim spared no detail when creating the body that appears before us now. Beginning up front, the fenders and headlights were lowered three inches from their original location. The fine horizontal bars of the grille are billet and were made by hand for this car.

Hinges for the doors were hidden from view to provide a seamless line that includes the smooth running boards. Rocker and quarter panels were also extended to bring more grace to the lines of the revised shape, and the body sits three inches lower over the rear chassis rails for a better stance. Turn signal lenses are frenched into the lower edges of the fenders to complete the theme. Even the rear license plate has been integrated into the lines of car to keep things smooth.

The convertible top was chopped three inches as well, so when it's in place, it does nothing to take away from the car that rests beneath it. When stowed behind-the-seats, a custom-made aluminum tonneau cover can be taken from the trunk and attached to retain a super-clean profile.

Formed by hand, this aluminum air cleaner neatly hides the pair of Edelbrock four-barrel carbs that lie beneath.

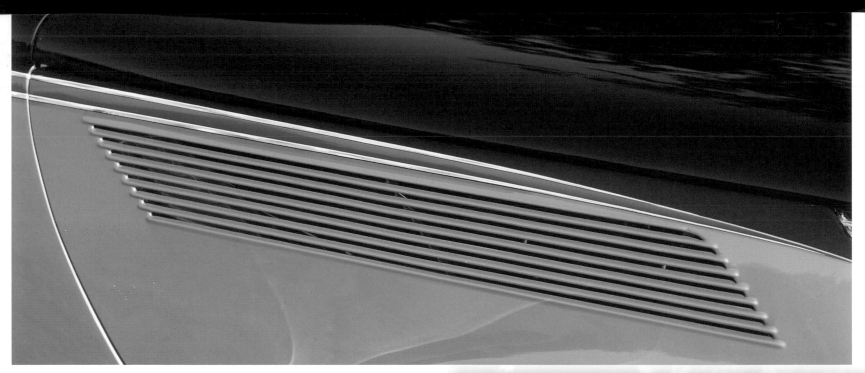

Doing double duty as functional and attractive, the hood louvers bring another fine touch of class to this radical rod.

Covering the expanse of sleek body panels is a combination of House of Kolor Black and a custom-blended Kandy Sunset Pearl. Separating the two contrasting colors is a tastefully applied streak of an alternate color and graphics. Jim's background in the use and application of color served him well on this rod, and a bevy of "best paint" awards decorates the walls of his garage.

As expected, the interior of the car received the same level of attention as the rest of the build. The wraparound dashboard was crafted specifically for this car as were the door panels that carry the ducts for the air conditioning in discretion. Continuing the secretive nature of the design, the shifter for the transmission is also tucked under the dashboard, keeping things tidy.

The seating is comprised of cut-down perches covered in Canyon-colored Garrett leather by Schober's Trim & Upholstery. Electronic controls for the air-ride suspension are concealed within the padded armrest, and the audio system is also hidden from view. Classic brand instruments were installed in the dash and a Lecarra steering wheel is held in a multitude of positions by the Iditit tilt column.

Heating and cooling are the responsibility of the Vintage Air components neatly mounted within the confines of the cockpit. The winged logos that are stitched into the upper portions of the seats are mirrored in chrome on the removable tonneau cover. It is the use of small detail such as this that sets this hot rod apart from its rivals. Having been featured as one of the few cars on the 2005 House of Kolors calendar doesn't hurt its reputation either.

It may have taken Jim 20 years to begin work on this car, but his efforts and painstaking attention to every detail made it well worth the wait.

Taillights and turn signals are all frenched-in for a clean look while providing the safety function they were intended to deliver.

1929 FORD COUPE

Owner: Tom Plunkett
Builder: NA

In the realm of hot rodding, there is only one rule, and that is there are no rules. A person can hot rod any type of car he desires, even if his plans fall outside the typical lines of convention. The '32 Ford has earned a place in the hot rod hall of fame, and its classic lines can be seen from a mile away. The 1929 Ford is not quite as common a platform when for hot rods.

When choosing a classic-bodied car for their hot rod project, many people immediately remove several inches from the roof and body height. This chopping results in a radically altered configuration, and lends itself more strongly to the custom market. Choosing another path for this car, the factory roof and body dimensions remain unaltered. The once-open roof has been filled in with steel, and fresh drip rails were added, but no other alterations to the sheet metal were made. A new and much stronger floor was added to keep things rigid and in line. After these mild modifications were made, the five-window body was coated with DuPont Sunset Copper paint.

The basic design of the car, along with the use of a single paint color, creates a strong visual statement when lined up with the cars fitted with chopped and channeled bodywork. Sometimes no change can make a stronger argument than a radical transformation.

Inside the factory body, we find an interior that blends the best of yesterday and today. The 1929 dashboard has been retained in its original form, but is painted to match the shell. It carries a set of Auto Meter gauges. An alloy, three-spoke steering wheel from Grant is mounted to the end of a tilt column for modern convenience. A Dodge minivan gave up one of its bench seats, which was then upholstered in sand-colored vinyl.

All the Ford window glass has also been upgraded to newer safety material. The floor of the cabin is uncluttered and carries nothing more than a simple, yet elegant shift lever, a brake and accelerator pedal. Contemporary carpeting covers every square inch of the sturdy floor that lies beneath.

Another modern adaptation is the application of the tilt column and Grant alloy steering wheel.

Mounted in the original 1929 dash is a set of Auto Meter gauges for modern day accuracy in an old world setting.

Using custom hairpins and torsion bars, the front axle is a work of art that works.

In its previous life, the bench seat resided in a Dodge Caravan but looks much cooler in this well-done rod.

They are a flash from the past—the Torque Thrust wheels from American Racing. The matte finish on the five gray spokes is complimented by the shine of the rims.

Carrying this mixture of new and old is a chassis from a 1932 Ford that was built by Steve's Automotive Fabrication. The rails are pinched to meet with the narrower dimensions of the '29 body. Hung from the front of the frame rails is a front axle complete with custom hairpins and a specially built torsion bar configuration. Ten-inch-diameter ventilated Wilwood disc brakes are on board and provide up-to-date braking on this vintage rod. Classic Torque Thrust wheels from American Racing are 15 x 4.5 inches and hold the Kleber tires tightly in place. Bringing up the rear we find a custom four-link suspension complete with Carrera coil-over shocks. Another pair of Wilwood 10-inch discs grace the back axle, as do slightly larger (15 x 8.5-inch) American Racing Torque Thrust wheels. B. F. Goodrich rubber was stretched over the aft hoops.

All of the best running gear means little without a potent mo-tor in the equation. Filling the bill in this case is a 1970 Chevrolet 350-cubic-inch mill. Inside the factory block you'll find a 3.48 inch stroke, Eagle connecting rods and forged pistons. A competition cam is monitored by Magnum rollers for consistent rpm delivery.

A Holley 650-fm carburetor is fed by an electric fuel pump from the same manufacturer and pulls from a 14-gallon custom fuel tank. A matching General Motors 350 Turbo transmission is bolted on for gear selection. Once selected, the chosen ratio is delivered to an eight-inch Ford rear end with a 10-inch converter and 3000-rpm stall. A stainless steel dual exhaust system flows through a pair of double chamber mufflers from Flowmaster.

Tom's wife often drives this car when they take both of his rods to an event. Her only complaint is that the rear wheels spin too easily, but that's not something that most hot rod guys would call a problem.

A Four-bar suspension is also installed on the front axle, along with custom hairpins and torsion bars for control.

It's nothing too wild, but the Chevrolet 350 will break the rear tires loose with nary a care, even with the slightest application of throttle.

1948 CHEVROLET PICKUP

Owner/Builder: Jeff Kuhn

With a long-time desire to own a cool pickup, Jeff's wife was given this 1948 Chevy eight years ago as a gift. It was delivered in its factory condition, and could have been restored to original specifications or taken to the hot rod level. The results we see here make her decision obvious, and it took a little less than a decade to complete the transformation. If Jeff had dropped it off at a shop and picked it up upon completion, the time span would have been shorter, but he did a bulk of the work himself. The end product looks every bit a high-end custom, but carries with it the pedigree of a true home-built hot rod.

Beginning the project with an existing truck offers several choices, as well as many new components that need to be crafted. Jeff designed and built the chassis for the '48 by himself and the construction is boxed from front to rear. This provides a neat appearance as and adds rigidity to the vehicle. The Heidt's suspension was melded to the front rails of the frame, and the truck carries a pair of Wilwood's four-piston calipers.

The entire assembly was polished to a rich luster before slipping on the 17-inch Magneato wheels from Boyd Coddington's collection. Continental 215/45ZR-17 rubber brings control and a quiet ride. The tail end of the frame holds a four-link suspension complete with Air Ride Technology height control. When parking the truck, Jeff hits the button and the entire truck drops to its knees like an obedient dog. Another set of four-piston calipers from Wilwood handles the rear braking duties and a slightly larger, 20-inch set of Boyd's Magneato rims hold the 245/45ZR-20 Continental donuts in place. As expected, every inch of the rear suspension has also been polished within an inch of its life.

Lurking beneath the hood you'll find a 502-cubic-inch monster from Chevrolet. The required machine work and final assembly fell into the hands of the owner, so we can understand why it took so

A minimalist set of gauges from Classic adorn the bright red dash from Hot Rod Hardware.

Poking its head out of the wooden rails of the truck bed we find the stainless steel fuel cap used to gain access to the tank that lies beneath.

You won't find much in the way of cargo in the bed, but the polished rails and sleek wooden slats are fully capable of holding a load of drywall.

Wanting as much "go" as "show" in his wife's truck, Jeff shoehorned a Chevrolet 502-cubic-inch V-8 in between the rails of the frame.

Upon opening the door of the cab, you are assaulted by the flaming red leather that covers nearly every inch of the cockpit. Dyed in the brightest red offered, the front seats offer plenty of comfort along with their alarming hue.

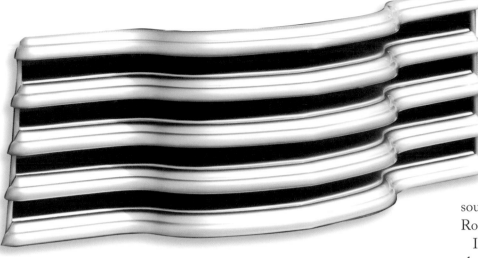

Dressed in a single hue of silver, and touting a shortened bumper, when dropped to the ground the front grille takes on an entirely new appearance.

long to finish this build. The electronic fuel injection hails from Street and Performance and metes out the needed fuel with precision. Keeping the inbound air free of debris is the K&N air cleaner, while the pulleys are also from Street and Performance.

A GM 700R4 transmission provides the driver with a selection of gears. The chosen ratio is delivered to a Ford 9-inch rear end that also carries Positraction and 3.50 gearing. The 2-1/2- inch stainless steel exhaust system winding below the truck was hand-formed by Jeff. A set of Flowmaster mufflers keep the noise level to a dull roar. Polished brake lines are another bit of Jeff's magic beneath the truck. Anything less would seem like a shortcut.

Riding majestically above this painted-and-polished drive train is the slick silver bodywork of the '48 Chevy truck. Although the stock dimensions of the cab were retained, numerous other alterations were made to the sheet metal. Hagan headlights peer from new frenched mountings and carry the turn signal lamps within the clear headlight lens assembly. The factory hood seam was welded smooth and the drip rails were removed from their former location to improve the sleek appearance.

Additional efforts to smooth the lines came from the now-missing cowl vent and a bumper that was shortened for a snug fit to the curves of the body.

The bed of the truck was trimmed with wooden rails and polished trim to retain some usefulness, but we doubt that Jeff hauls much lumber with this beauty. The stainless steel fuel tank can be filled by gaining access through the use of the in-bed fuel cap. DuPont silver paint covers every remaining inch of the truck's metal and is flawless in its execution. Getz's Hot Rod Innovations is responsible for that aspect of the truck and is well known for paint skills.

Open either door of the truck's cab and you are

greeted by acres of screaming red leather. No attempt was made to select a tamer shade and the effect is stunning. A Hot Rod Hardware dash is mounted with a set of Classic gauges along with Phipps air conditioning vents. The "Chicayne" steering wheel is a Billet Specialties product that is made to meet each customer's needs. Wool carpeting is also dyed in the same bright red to match the leather. All trim work was done by Schober's Trim and Upholstery. Not content to listen to the thumping sounds of the motor, a Kenwood audio system is powered by a pair of Rockford Fosgate amps that live behind the front seat.

It may have taken Jeff eight years to complete, his truck but it has already taken home trophies and awards from some of the biggest shows in the country. Good things do take time, and this project is a perfect example of that.

Replacing the ribbed, black rubber units found on the original truck, the running boards are now seamless steel for an uncluttered look.

The five-window design of the 1940s truck remains a classic today and also provides extra visibility for the driver.

1932 FORD HI-BOY

Owner: Scott Bischoff
Builder: J.R. Carnes

Within the pages of this publication, we have chosen to illustrate a small sampling of what owners can do when building a '32 Ford. With that year, make and model being as popular as it is, there is literally no end to the variations that can be created. We have shown you a few cars that were designed and built to the owner's exacting requirements, but this hi-boy was more of a happy bit of good luck.

Scott has owned several hot rods with his dad over the years, and there were times when the garage was devoid of anything exciting. With a few major hurdles having been jumped, he decided to re-enter the world of hot rods and ownership of a 1932 Ford. As luck would have it, a friend of his had just returned from a road trip that took him through Tennessee.

Facing the prospect of returning to Illinois with an empty trailer, his friend purchased a '32 Ford he had stumbled upon and carted it home. Once home, he called Scott to share the news. The stars must have been in perfect alignment. Scott revealed his desire to buy a '32 Ford Ford the same week this one had arrived. A deal was made and Scott now had the '32 Ford Ford he wanted in his garage.

J. R. Carnes has earned a reputation for building hot rods down in Tennessee, and this clean '32 is a great cross section of his work. Beginning with a Rat Glass body, he added a Hercules three-section steel hood and grille shell. The vertical bars of the stainless steel insert made the perfect accent for the contours of the shell. A rolled rear pan added a touch of sleekness to the aft of the car. Once the contours of the body were smoothed to perfection, General Motors Shell Metallic paint was used to cover the surfaces. DuPont clearcoat was applied before rubbing the entire mix to a glass-like smoothness.

Carriage Works sold the steering wheel that was then mounted to an Ididit tilt-column for convenience.

An Alan Johnson air cleaner cover hides the efficient K&N air filter that lies beneath it.

A Pete and Jake's four-bar front end is joined with a four-inch drop axle combining modern day metallurgy with old world hardware.

Keeping the driver informed is this set of VDO gauges tucked into the Rat Glass dashboard.

Looking like something borrowed from a WW I fighter plane, the divided window frame holds tinted glass in style.

Ricky Bendinelli handled the almost imperceptible pinstriping.

The cockpit of the car borders on austere, but is well equipped with everything a rodder could need. Mounted into the Rat Glass dashboard is an assembly of VDO gauges, that keep the driver apprised of critical temperatures, speed and pressures. The tilt column came from Ididit, and is mated to a Nostalgia steering wheel from Carriage Works. Lokar was chosen for the shift lever, gas and brake pedals.

The bench seat was custom built for the car before being covered in purple-gray faux leather. Juliano's seat belts add a modicum of safety to a car that lacks any form of roof support. Devoid of an audio system, the driver and passenger are free to enjoy the purring motor and the sounds of the open road passing beneath them. Looking through the DuVall-style windshield, complete with modern tinted glass, eases the eyestrain and provides some protection from the breeze.

Besides having the road beneath them, a chassis from Bobby Alloway, complete with a Deuce Factory spreader-bar, holds the show together. The Pete and Jake's catalog was worked over when choosing the four-bar front end and the four-inch dropped-tube axle. Dynalite disc brakes from Wilwood are matched with polished billet calipers to slow the car. The Pete and Jakes offerings were again used to assemble the rear four-bar suspension system that is controlled by Viper coil-over shocks. A Chevy, 10-bolt rear end was selected and fitted with 3.23 gearing that can be easily swapped through the use of the quick-change cover.

Rolling stock comes from American Racing with a four pack of their Torque Thrust II wheels. Size 15 x 6-inches were installed up front with more aggressive 17 x 9-1/2 inches at the rear. B. F. Goodrich Comp T/A tires provide grip and a comfortable ride.

Leaving the best for last, we look under the hood and find a small block Chevy mill that displaces 305 cubic inches. A Carter AFB Competition Series four-barrel carburetor draws in 500-cfm through a mechanical fuel pump. Tanks, Inc. was leaned on for the storage container. The aerodynamic air cleaner is the work of Alan Johnson and incorporates the workings of a K&N filter within. A Chevy 350 Turbo gearbox is bolted to the rear of the motor and provides three-speeds without hesitation.

Although purchased as-is, Scott brings the spirit of hot rodding to any event he attends when he rolls in with his '32 hi-boy. Although Scott didn't build this car himself, he uses it as often as he can, and that's what these cars were made for, regardless of who screws them together.

1950 MERCURY COUPE "MAVERICK MERC"

Owner: Gerald W. Grupe
Builder: Midwest Hot Rods

When Gerry was only 17 years old, he built his first 1949 custom. Starting with a four-door sedan, he frenched the headlights, added a rolled-and-pleated interior and bolted in a 301-cid engine from a '56 Chevrolet. He built the car in 1957, sold it in 1959 and vowed to one day build a second Mercury to replace his first love. It wouldn't be until 1990, but Gerry would make up for lost time when he had this "Maverick Merc" created.

A growing business found Gerry in a better place financially, so when the day came to build another custom Merc, he turned to Midwest Hot Rods to have most of the time-consuming body modifications made. The two-door body was chopped by three inches at the front and 3-1/2 inches at the rear. To conform to the new height of the roof, the "B" pillars and door posts were laid down at a more rakish angle. The corners of these components were then rounded off for a smoother appearance. The corners of the hood were also rounded and any unsightly body seams were filled and smoothed.

Like his first car, the headlights of this Merc were frenched in and a floating grille from a 1957 Corvette was added to the opening. Both front and rear bumpers were molded into the body and the rear license plate is hidden from view, but appears at the touch of a button. Forgetting the plate so has gotten Gerry pulled over by local police more than once. The taillights and front turn signals were all custom made for the car before being flush mounted into the seamless body panels. The rear pan was rolled and molded into the body as well. No exterior chrome remains and the Candy Apple Plum and anodized paint received six coats of clear for a mirrored, high-gloss finish.

After being stripped of the factory chrome and glitz, the dash was trimmed with a billet instrument panel and covered in purple leather and hopsack.

When Jerry had this Mercury built initially, it was 1990. He has since redone the entire interior and upgraded every surface. His 1998 do-over included front bucket seats borrowed from a 1977 Cadillac Eldorado that were reduced in height plus a hand-made rear seat. The full-length center console was mirrored with the overhead unit that houses the electric window and radar detector controls. A reflective surface was applied to this overhead trough and adds a dimension of size to the cozy cockpit. The factory Mercury dashboard was gone over, and every hint of chrome was removed.

A billet insert carries a complete set of eight VDO gauges in a neat and tidy fashion. For his aural pleasure, a Sony "Stackman" CD-AM/FM-cassette unit was slipped into the sweeping console, just to the right of the steering wheel. Six speakers fill the interior with sound when called upon and the Mercury glass was supplanted with tinted safety plate. A Cadillac tilt column is topped off with a custom wheel, and every surface of the cabin is covered in either hopsack or leather, both in shades of purple.

The 1950 Mercury frame was modified and bolstered to carry the latest in high-powered running gear. To accommodate the wider rear meats, the chassis rails were narrowed by seven inches. Gerry wanted his new Mercury custom to roll with a lower stance, but was loath to compromise the ride quality. To achieve both goals, the front suspension uprights were truncated, removing three inches from the car's height with no loss of comfort.

Inside the car we find a sweeping console that carries the audio system controls and continues unabated to the rear seats.

Ensconced safely in the long billet housing we find eight different VDO gauges keeping the driver fully informed.

Looking like kissing cousins to the cut down Eldorado seats used up front, the rear seats were actually handmade for the car before being swaddled in purple leather.

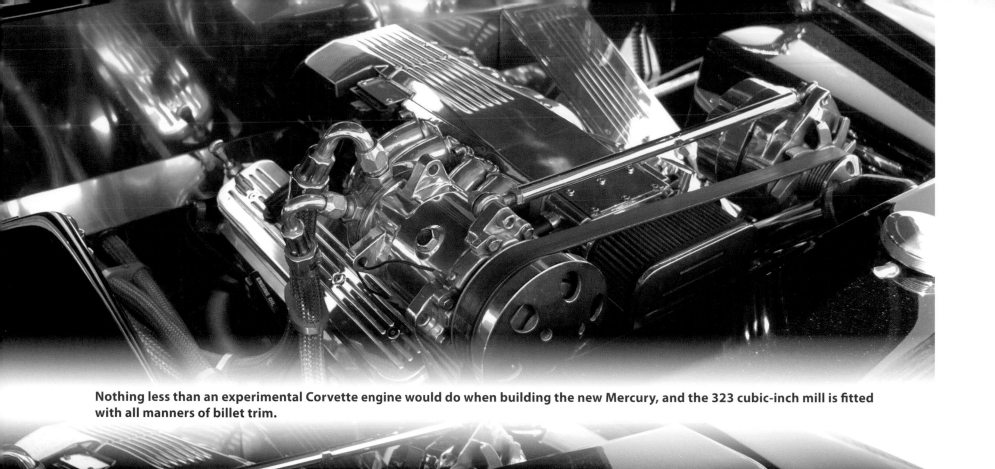

Nothing less than an experimental Corvette engine would do when building the new Mercury, and the 323 cubic-inch mill is fitted with all manners of billet trim.

Keeping the NASCAR radiator from view is this sheet metal cowl that was built to include the winged mascot of the Mercury line.

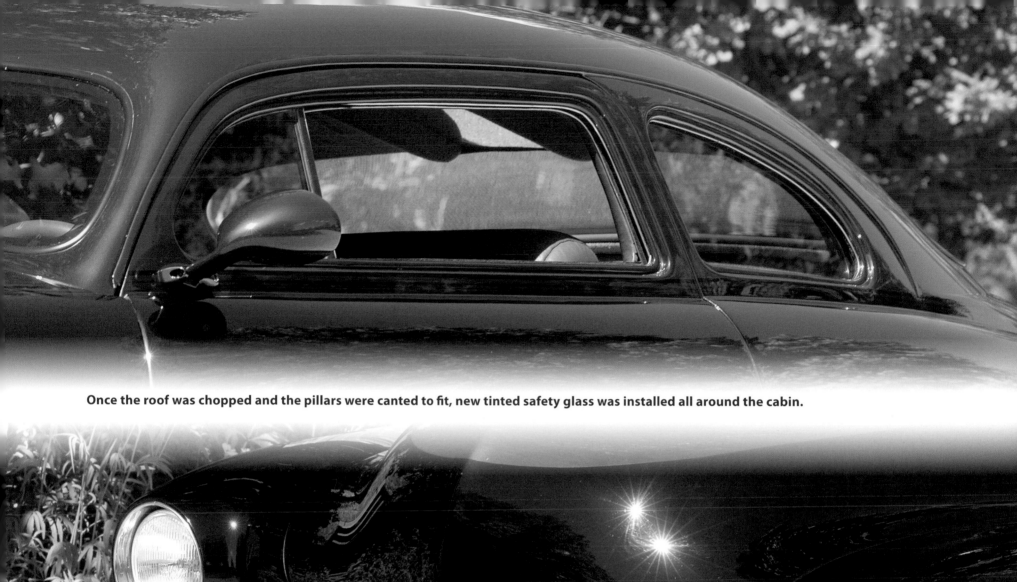

Once the roof was chopped and the pillars were canted to fit, new tinted safety glass was installed all around the cabin.

With the front bumper molded into the fenders and a 1957 Corvette grille suspended in the opening, the Mercury front end has never looked so sleek.

From the molded rear bumper to the hidden license plate, the aft end of this Mercury is stealthy to say the least.

The new motor caused some clearance questions, so the steering arms and tie rod assembly were modified along with a drag link to provide safe steering without hitting the oil pan of the new mill. The front cross member was also modified and carries a Ford F-100 power steering box on a custom bracket. Front braking is achieved by having the Plymouth Volare rotors grabbed by Chevrolet Camaro calipers. A Lincoln Versailles rear axle was joined by a Wilwood disc brake arrangement and carries a 3.90 rear end complete with Positraction. The rear sway bar was taken from a Chevrolet S-10 pickup that also required special mounting hardware.

Powering this custom Mercury down the road is an experimental Corvette engine from 1990. The exotic mill features aluminum heads and a roller-tappet cam and displaces 323 cubic inches. A contemporary fuel-injection system sips from a vintage Mercury fuel tank, assisted by a Corvette in-tank pump, accumulator and screen. Street & Performance were contacted for the serpentine belt system and aluma-coat headers. The radiator was crafted using a NASCAR core with a double set of coils. Engine and transmission coolers were also added and draw breath through hand made air scoops. A 700R4 automatic transmission delivers the gear ratios smoothly and all major components of the motor can be serviced using the Chevrolet parts catalog.

It may have taken Gerry more than 50 years to rekindle his Mercury dream, but a room full of industry-leading trophies and magazine coverage made the wait worthwhile.

Alloy rims roll at all points and are 16 inches in diameter, going against the grain of today's 20-inch monsters.

1932 FORD THREE-WINDOW COUPE

Owner/Builder: Tom Plunkett

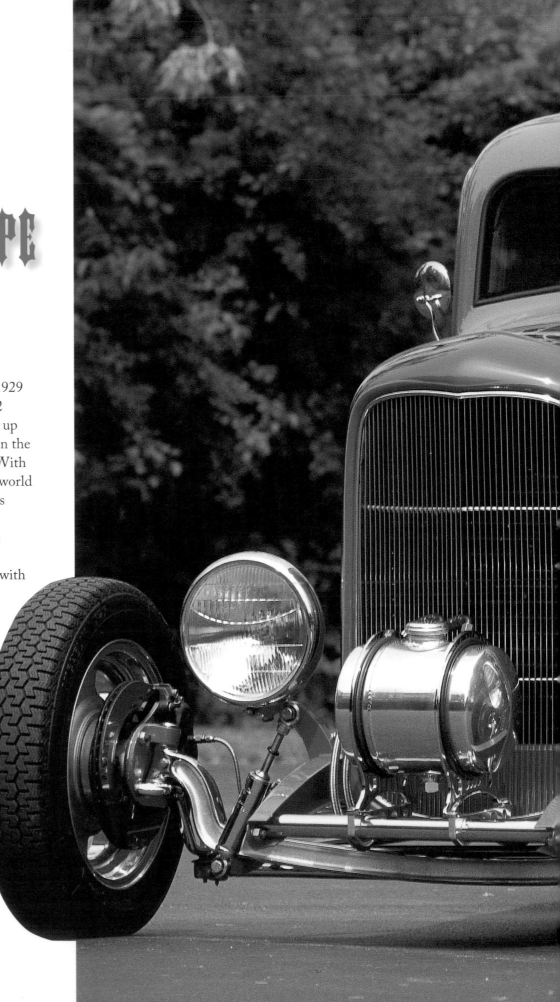

With an empty spot in his immaculate garage, and his 1929 Ford getting lonely, Tom decided to build a classic '32 Ford coupe to keep it company. With his mind made up as to what kind of car he would build next, Tom began the search for the components needed to complete the assembly. With 1932 Fords being one of hot rodding's favorite cars, there is a world of choices for anyone wanting to put one togethe. So he set his sights on the combination that best suited his needs.

A chassis from TCI was ordered, and then pinched by three inches to accommodate the rest of the hardware. A four-inch dropped axle from Pete & Jake's was installed up front, along with the standard four-bar controls. Wilwood was tapped for the 10-inch diameter brake discs and matching calipers.

A set of modern Billet Specialties five-opening wheels were added to the mix to keep things in the right frame of mind. The 15 x 4-1/2-inch rims were wrapped with 145/15 rubber from Goodyear. The rear end, complete with a Ford eight-inch pumpkin, is suspended by a set of Carrera coil-over shocks with Ford anchors at each wheel.

Another set of Billet Specialties five-opening wheels, this time measuring 17 x 9-1/2 inches, were also covered with Goodyear donuts. The bigger 275/60-17 rubber does what it can to keep the tires from breaking loose under heavy throttle.

Attached to the gas pedal is a Chevrolet 355-cubic-inch engine that draws fuel through a Holley 650-cfm carburetor. A mechanical pump from General Motors feeds from the Rock Valley storage tank helps keep the

Although mounted to a stock '32 dash, the VDO gauges keep the driver up to date with accurate measurements of all vital functions.

While other portions of the car are loaded with modern contrivances, the taillights are straight off a 1932 Ford.

A symbol of modern convenience is the custom Lobeck wheel mounted at the end of a tilt column.

Modern Wilwood disc brakes pull the car down from speed up front and are assisted by Ford drums at the rear.

The molded door panels are a touch of today to compliment the cabin that blends old and new in a subtle fashion.

Looking like something borrowed from a top fuel race car, the aluminum tank holds the precious fuel in safety.

The four-inch dropped axle is kept in check by the chrome four-bar suspension.

A full length dual exhaust system can be seen along with a painted and polished roll pan and paintedrunning gear.

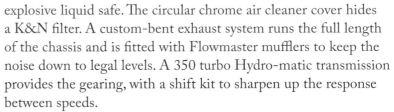

explosive liquid safe. The circular chrome air cleaner cover hides a K&N filter. A custom-bent exhaust system runs the full length of the chassis and is fitted with Flowmaster mufflers to keep the noise down to legal levels. A 350 turbo Hydro-matic transmission provides the gearing, with a shift kit to sharpen up the response between speeds.

The car's body was chopped three inches before being dropped onto the narrow frame rails. Colors selected for the car were not trying to appear subtle. The PPG Ford Orange was trimmed with the Candy Green and Blue flames, then outlined in a bright blue. It should be a law that anyone building a '32 rod is required to apply flames to the vehicle, and Tom's choice of colors adds a new dimension to the timeless tradition. A Walker radiator hides behind the painted shell and a fine set of stainless fins keep the architecture classic.

Opening either suicide door of the '32 reveals a tasteful blend of old and new school design. The spacious bench seat, borrowed from a Dodge minivan, is now upholstered in tweed and vinyl for comfort and convenience. The stock dashboard now carries an up-to-date set of instruments from VDO that are a bit more accurate than the factory units they replaced. Further interior enhancements include the air conditioning and heating system, joined by power windows for the more moderate days.

A tilt steering column provides easier entrance and exit for the driver and a Lobek wheel compliments the balance of the cabin. For the times when the melodious sounds from the engine bay aren't enough, the Alpine AM/FM/CD stereo sends its high-quality sound through a system of speakers. Modern-day, tinted glass has replaced the factory panes for safety and clarity.

Exterior lighting on this new-millennium rod hails from the original 1932 Ford. The taillights sweep upwards gracefully on a set of chrome stalks, holding the lamps in place with style.

There's no telling when Tom's collection will grow again, but we can be sure whatever car joins the group; it'll be done with the same attention to detail as the two we've seen in this book.

1940 FORD WOODIE

Owner/Builder: Jim Talaga

One needn't look too deeply into the archives of hot rodding to find a number of references to the classic "woodie." Whether in the world of rock and roll or vintage vehicles, the car is named for its wooden construction and classic design. While woodies are often restored to their former glory, there are some owners who take their cars in another direction.

Jim's wife, Pat, was originally exposed to the woodies when her father drove one back in the day. She carried fond memories of long road trips in the car, and these recollections earned it a place in her heart. When the desire to build another hot rod came into play, Jim chose this rare 1940 Ford as the basis for his new project. Fewer than 9,000 copies of this model were built for the 1940 model year, and the nature of their assembly has left only a handful in existence today.

Beginning with a fairly decent car, Jim removed the body and boxed in sections of the frame rails where required. The added strength comes in handy when Jim install more muscular motor and running gear. The fortified chassis was fitted with a Mustang front suspension from Heidt's and a two-inch dropped axle carrying matching dropped spindles. General Motors disc brakes were mounted to each end of the axle for confident stopping. A Chevrolet rear end was added. The suspension was provided with a set of Posie springs. Chevy drum brakes help to slow the big car down. Kelly tires keep all four of the Boyd Coddington rims off the macadam and deliver a quiet ride on long trips.

When the car was built by Ford in 1940, only an 85 horsepower V-8 was available under the hood. Although dependable in its day, it is not something that hot rod builders dream of. With durability and horsepower as two of his major criteria, Jim swapped out the original mill for a Chevrolet 350 cubic-inch model. The fresh

Although bearing modern safety glass, the original two-part windshield has been retained.

In an effort to create a car that would be comfortable during long drives, the factory dash has been augmented with several modern conveniences.

The expansive roof of the cabin has also been refinished to a gleaming luster.

Bringing the car up to contemporary standards meant adding a working air conditioning unit, and it has been expertly integrated into a custom made lower dash section by O'Connell Specialties.

Something old in something new, the 1940 door handles have been carried over into the contemporary rebuild.

Every inch of the car's wood has been refinished for longevity and terrific looks.

motor drinks through a four-barrel carburetor with 16 gallons of fuel on board when filled to the brim. A Holley fuel pump ensures the delivery is smooth and uninterrupted. Two-inch diameter tubing was selected for the exhaust system and a pair of stainless mufflers keeps the woodie quiet enough for early morning surf runs. Having addressed his durability and power requirements, Jim opted to add a set of billet pulleys and air cleaner for some added flash. A 200R transmission delivers the proper ratios to the rear end without hesitation.

When building their woodie, Jim and Pat wanted to be sure it would make for comfortable rides when traveling long distances. To achieve this goal, a wide variety of improvements were made to the spacious interior of the car.

With every inch of the wood refinished, the stock seats, all three of them, were recovered in a combination of black Hartz cloth and tan naugahyde. A tilt steering column from the General Motors parts bin was joined by a Lecarra steering wheel for a touch of modern day elegance. The stock dashboard was enhanced by adding a lower section to carry the newly installed air conditioner in a fashion that belies its custom nature. O'Connell Specialties was responsible for that bit of trickery, giving us a brief glimpse at their range of abilities. The A/C and heating units were provided by Vintage Air. The factory dash has also been upgraded by the installation of VDO gauges within the original ports.

To make long road trips more pleasurable, cruise control was also thrown into the electronic web. A fully modern Alpine audio system plays any form of music you please, including surfer tunes from the 1960s. New glass was installed all around the vehicle to improve both vision and safety.

The outer skin of the woodie features completely refurbished wood and PPG black lacquer. An acre or so of black Hartz cloth was used to re-cover the expansive roof that looks like it have been there since 1940. The paint and finish of the woodie have earned it numerous awards and trophies since its completion.

Once the car was completed, Pat was quickly reminded why the woodie had been her favorite car as a child. The classic charm of the wooden body, joined with up-to-date running gear, makes this car a favorite.

Carried on the rear door as Henry Ford intended it, the spare tire is easy to access in the event of a flat on the open road.

1932 FORD CABRIOLET

Owner/Builder: Jim Talaga

Even as a younger man, Jim Talaga had dreams of one day owning and driving a 1932 Ford cabriolet. The day finally dawned in 1981. The purchase allowed Jim to build his first hot rod. Having only limited working space, Jim painted and built this entire car in a two-car garage. He did nearly every facet of the work himself.

Work on his dream hot rod began by removing the body and boxing in sections of the frame for stiffness. When originally built, these cars were powered by engines with far less than 100 horsepower, and didn't need any additional rigidity. Once a higher horsepower engine is installed, all kinds of troubles begin especially if throttle is used with any aggression. With the frame rails reinforced, he modified the front cross member to accept the modern power plant. A four-inch dropped axle was added to the front of the rails and the spring eyes were reversed to alter the mounting position of the M-G lever arm shocks.

Somewhat generic disc brakes were then bolted on from a General Motors vehicle to provide the required stopping power. Between the rear frame rails, a Ford nine-inch rear end was mounted with a set of Chevrolet Corvair coil springs and another set of M-G lever arm shocks. Ford drum brakes were used in the fight to bring the car down from velocity. Wire wheels, taken from a 1978 Cadillac, were mounted with Goodyear rubber, 165 series up front and larger 275 on the rear. Triple-bladed spinners, complete with Corvair spider inserts, cap off each glistening wheel.

Now that Jim had his rolling chassis completed, it was time for an engine. Some builders are happy with a simple Chevy 350 small-block under the hood, as well they should be, but Jim had other plans. With a desire to keep his car all Ford, he selected a 302-cubic-inch V-8 from that

Often referred to as a "mother-in-law'" seat, the folding rumble seat disappears into the rear half of the car when not in use.

Another non-Ford component is the 1968 Chevelle steering wheel and tilt column.

Affixed to the face of the standard Ford dash is this alloy panel that holds the instruments neatly in line.

Looking every bit the race engine, the 302 Ford V-8 is topped off with a hand-made air cleaner assembly complete with eight velocity stacks.

maker. Since this car was a long-time dream for him, Jim wanted many aspects to be really different from what he'd seen on other '32 Fords.

A single Holley four-barrel carburetor was chosen for fuel delivery, but the air cleaner was something he made for this engine. The eight velocity stacks look like something straight off of a race engine, and add a new dimension to the under-the-hood excitement. Billet pulleys add some additional spice to the bay, but the air cleaner takes the prize. The stock Ford fuel tank is drained by a Holley electric fuel pump while a C4 transmission is in charge of the gears. A two-inch diameter exhaust system was bent to snake through the chassis' components, and stainless steel mufflers provide the sound deadening.

The steel body of the car was also modified to fit Jim's needs, with a lowered stance as his goal. The top was chopped by two inches and the bows of the cabriolet roof were modified to meet with the profile he envisioned. To match the new reduced height of the body and roof, the headlight bar was also lowered by two inches. House of Kolor Kandy Wine coats the sheet metal, while Mercedes burgundy was selected for the roof. The end result is both tasteful and exotic.

With the top folded back, we can get a better look at the interior, which has been treated to its own set of custom tricks and treats.

The stock Ford seat was cut down to match the lower profile of the body and was then upholstered by Jim Larson in the deep burgundy leather. The factory Ford dash was painted in the same Kandy Wine as the body and fitted with elongated alloy face plate. Then, the Stewart Warner gauges were slipped into place. One of the only non-Ford bits on the car is the 1968 Chevelle tilt column and steering wheel. Another Corvair Spyder is mounted in the center of the horn button. This assembly is tied to a Ford Econoline van steering box with cross-steering layout.

Wanting a car he could drive in almost any weather, air conditioning and heat were added via a Vintage Air system mounted beneath the dash. Alpine electronics provide any music that Jim and his wife would like to hear. The only person who might miss out on the comfort and music would be seated in the rumble seat, otherwise known as a "mother-in-law" chair. The upholstery of the hideaway seat is the same rich leather as that used in the cabin.

Halogen lighting was installed at both ends of the car for safety, and gray-tinted glass was used at all points.

It took Jim two years to build this hot rod, but considering that he did 99 percent of the work himself, and that he has since won numerous trophies and awards with the car, we'd say he did pretty well for a guy in his own garage.

With the inner bows modified to lower the height and contour of the roof, the resulting top conforms to the revised body more gracefully.

A set of wire wheels from a 1978 Cadillac is one of the few things on the car that doesn't hail from Ford. Finishing off the sparkling wire wheels are three-bladed spinners with Corvair Spyder inserts.

1937 FORD TUDOR

Owner: Bill Baron
Re-Builder: O' Connell Specialties

Bill Baron has owned several hot rods through the years with an ever-increasing appetite for cooler machines. His collection currently includes this 1937 Ford along with a 1954 Chevrolet seen elsewhere in this book. Diversification is king, but Bill's demand for his cars to be as fast as they are amazing is a benchmark that he holds the builders to when they put the cars together. This project ended up at Tim O'Connell's shop for rebuilding and completion, and Bill was able to drive the deal home.

The full-fendered 1937 Ford Tudor is hardly a svelte car to begin with, so Bill had some changes made to lessen the overall mass of its appearance. When the lift-off roof is in place, it rides with a profile that is 2-1/2 inches lower than the factory's design. Covering the revised one-piece unit in a light-colored fabric helps to keep the appearance cleaner, and not as bulbous. A few quick releases of the inside latches and the car is now a convertible.

The tall front grille of the Ford was originally finished in bright chrome, but Bill opted for a color-matched Pearl White hue for the delicate vanes that make up the assembly. Tri-bar headlights from a vintage Jaguar are found deeply frenched into the curvaceous fenders, just one of many beautiful details. A slender, single section bumper provides the needed protection while retaining a sleek profile. Small turn signal lamps are found in compliance with governmental regulations for such things.

A custom-formed hood covers the tidy engine bay and it, along with the top section of the body, is painted in a glamorous Bronze Champagne hue that accents the Pearl White applied to the lower half. The seashell graphics are also a different way to decorate the car, and help to guide the eye away from the otherwise massive steel panels. The power trunk lid is also covered in the Bronze Champagne paint and leads us to a trio of elliptical taillight lenses and large diameter chrome exhaust outlets. Another sliver of a bumper was mounted to protect the tail section from slow-speed damage.

As if borrowed from the face shield of a space invader's helmet, this bank of Dakota Digital gauges is both informative and stylish.

The only stock thing about the cabin of this car is the space that holds the all-new dashboard, console and seats.

The console was built from scratch to carry the required electronic controls in style.

Another bit of new world is the electrically adjusted bucket seats taken from a Toyota, then ensconced in leather by Schober's.

Billet wipers swipe away any rain that has the nerve to fall on the car.

A hot rod is nothing without power, and this LT1 crate motor from Chevy does the job with horsepower to spare.

All of this revised sheet metal rides on a steel tube frame crafted from rectangular stock. Heidt's Mustang II suspension is mated to a power steering setup for ease of driving. General Motors disc brakes were installed on the front axle, allowing Bill to slow the big car without fear. A pair of Chassis Engineering leaf springs holds the rear axle in position, along with the Ford drum brakes. The all-steel driveline is joined by a Ford nine-inch rear end known for proven durability. French Michelin rubber is wrapped around the Boyd Coddington wheels beneath each fender, bringing a measure of contemporary custom to a vintage rod.

All the world's best bodywork means nothing without something healthy under the hood, at least that's the way Bill sees it. Powering this rod along in style is a Chevrolet LT1 crate motor. The 350 cubic inches are fed through a tuned-port injection system for efficiency and power on command. A General Motors 700R4 gearbox is stuffed with four speeds and an overdrive gear for comfortable highway cruising. There's not much sense in building a car that can't be taken anyplace you want to go.

A stainless 2-1/2-inch diameter exhaust system leads the spent fumes away, but not before they travel through a pair of Stainless Works mufflers to keep the peace.

The cabin of the car is as heavily modified as the rest, with Schober's Trim & Upholstery to blame for the butter-soft leather pulled over Toyota seats. The entire dashboard and vertical console assemblies were handcrafted before being stuffed with the latest in electronics. The space-age horizontal instrument band is the work of Dakota Digital A Pioneer audio unit compliments a Sony CD changer and Infinity speakers. Wanting a car that was capable of being driven in all manners of weather conditions, the '37 Bill packed with air conditioning, heat, power windows and seat adjustments. A Billet Specialties steering wheel caps off the festivities and is wrapped in leather to match the seats.

His laundry list of power, style and modern conveniences have all been checked-off on this car. The proof of the efforts can be seen as Bill rolls into car shows all around the country.

Twin Jaguar tri-bar headlights are recessed into the sweeping fenders offering the altered look of a classic.

While maintaining the regal dimensions of the original, Bill had the grille assembly painted to match the car for a seamless appearance.

Owner: Al & Leora Brockly
Builder: Various

Of all the cars in this book, this 1937 Willys carries with it the longest history of ownership as well as the most prestigious award. With his eyes set on doing some drag racing, Al Brockly bought this 1937 Willys 51 years ago for the princely sum of $35. Pressing the car into racing duty resulted in some expected bangs and dents. A few years later Al began searching for a replacement front clip for the car.

Having no luck in finding just the parts he needed, Al was forced to buy a second Willys for about $4,000. Paying that much for a car pained him, so he decided to sell off the parts he didn't need, to recoup his cost. After selling the balance of the car, he actually turned a profit of $35. This gave him a free car for this project. His decision to build a car worthy of winning the "Ridler Award" didn't come cheaply, but ended up being well worth the investment. It would take nearly 18 years for the car to reach the stage we see it in now, with the usual range of setbacks and disappointments along the way.

The Don Ridler Memorial Award is named for a fabled promoter who used his formidable abilities as a producer to expand the scope of the Detroit Autorama. This car show came to be in the 1950s. Following Don's death in 1963, a decision was made to award the coveted trophy in memory of his work. The range of cars that have earned the trophy is expansive. They stretch the limits of man's creativity and mechanical prowess.

After using the car in a number of drag racing efforts, Al grew weary of the toils and parked the car. After it sat for nearly 20 years, he decided to build a car worthy of the Ridler Award. This sort of dream doesn't come easily or cheaply, but Al has a history of doing everything at 110 mph.

Affixed to a custom-fabricated steel dash is a billet insert, along with a full bank of Dakota Digital gauges.

The Ididit steering column shields a chain-driven transfer case that operates a low, chassis-mounted steering box. This eliminates same typical clearance woes under the hood.

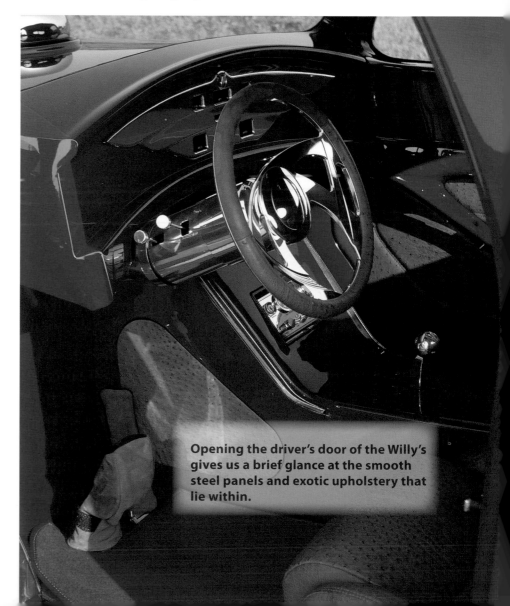

Opening the driver's door of the Willy's gives us a brief glance at the smooth steel panels and exotic upholstery that lie within.

One sweeping section of steel creates the center console. It is flanked by custom A/C vents and holds some of the car's electronic controls.

With his desire to create a car that was different from all the rest, Al chose ostrich and suede for his upholstered surfaces and wound up with stunning results.

To replace the standard chassis, Al had Dave Reeder fabricate a complete tubular frame using chrome-moly stock. After viewing the underside of this car at length, I can tell you it's almost a shame that the shapely body covers this truly remarkable work of art. Along with welds that belie their strength, the components crafted to assemble the rest of the frame are equally amazing. Each link in the rear-four-bar suspension is a gorgeous piece of tapered, contoured and highly polished sculpture.

Anything not polished to a perfect gleam has been painted in the same PPG Milano Red hue that covers the body. Not content to purchase an off-the-shelf rear axle, Al spent countless hours creating a mockup of his desired unit from cardboard. He then gave it to Tim O'Connell, of O'Connell Specialties, who then crafted the actual assembly from steel. The front suspension is equally exotic, with the entire independent arrangement being carved from billet aluminum. The fully-functional design, is one-of-a kind. Wilwood 11-inch disc brakes are mounted behind each of the Billet Specialties Cyclone wheels. The wheels themselves had a very limited run and are no longer produced. Mickey Thompson rubber keeps the shiny hoops off the pavement and provides plenty of traction.

The all-steel body is a combination of the original 1937 Willys that Al bought 51 years ago and a hood and grille taken from a 1941.

Stock headlight housings from the '41 were filled with modern LED lamps created by O'Connell Specialties. Some 1940 Ford fenders gave their lives to become the inner panels installed on the new Willys. The car's original drag racing heritage was honored by using a full roll cage within the interior sheet metal. With the bodywork completed by J&D Enterprises, Ron Kral was tapped to apply the PPG Milano Red paint.

The cockpit of this award winner is another mass of hand-built features all rolled into one seamless presentation. Every inch of the custom panels is steel and, as we mentioned, help to conceal the race-ready roll cage. Glide Engineering seats have been upholstered with a combination of ostrich and suede, with Schober's Trim Shop chosen for the task. Additional sections of this rare bird's hide have been installed in the door panels and footwells to continue the theme.

The steel dashboard contains more custom work, and carries an O'Connell Specialties billet insert that is loaded with Dakota Digital instruments. The sweeping center console carries more electronics, as well as the vertical air conditioning ducts that grace each flank of the assembly. An Ididit steering column holds the Billet Specialties wheel in place, and its rim has been covered in a combination of ostrich and suede.

When this much attention is paid to every detail under and inside the car, one doesn't expect shortcuts to be taken in the engine compartment. With drag racing in his blood, Al selected a Donovan Engineering, 355-cubic-inch mill for his Willys. Feeding the alloy block is a joint effort between the Weiand/GMC 6-71 supercharger and the Hilborn injection that lies directly beneath it. This old-school combination is assembled from some vintage components along with up-to-date technology. Every inch of the assembled power plant has been polished, and the valve covers bear the Willys insignia in their gleaming surfaces.

Al never saw this project taking nearly two decades to complete, but from the start had wanted the car to be built his way, and with the Ridler Award as his target. His persistence was rewarded in 2004 when the Willys brought home the Ridler Award, along with the accolades that go with of that momentous trophy.

Al owned portions of the Hilborn injection system since he was 17 years old. Hillborn offered to buy the vintage unit from him, but he preferred using it in his award-winning Willys.

1934 FORD COUPE

Owner: Dan DeLara and Dan De Lara Jr.
Builder: Guy Stone

Another car in this book that carries a bit of history behind it is this 1934 Ford coupe. It was first built between the years of 1961 and 1965, after which it took to the show car circuit. By 1968 it had become a huge hit with show goers, and toured heavily as a feature vehicle. In 1969 it was retired from the series, and put away in a garage. The car was not built to be driven in the '60s, it was purely a show vehicle. Dan DeLara and his son bought the car from a relative in 1998, and re-built it to become the very drivable car you see here.

The original car was created using an all-steel body, then the roof was chopped by four inches and the body "cheater sectioned" by six inches. The front end features a hand-formed radiator grille with a shape that mimicked the rear of the car. The rear housing also carries a set of custom fabricated tubing to form a grille of sorts. One of the more unusual features of the car is the offset aluminum panel that is set into the sheet metal. It runs the full length of the vehicle. The rear segment hinges upward to reveal the gas filler cap that hides beneath.

A small chrome grille also hides the mandatory third brake light mounted to the rear of the cabin. Originally painted in kind of a candy orange hue, Dan and his son chose a shade of PPG white that was contrasted by a fading House of Kolor Purple Passion accent stripe. The result is something that would look right at home on the cover of a Beach Boys album. Guy Stone was employed to do the 1998 mods. The first set of sheet metal shapes were hammered out by Dave Puhl back in the 1960s.

Underneath the newly-painted body is an original 1934 Ford chassis that was box sectioned by Guy Stone in the second build. A four-inch dropped front axle from Chassis Engineering is held in position by a Posies four-bar linkage and a set of Wilwood disc brakes are trimmed by Zipper decorative covers.

The alloy trim panel runs the length of the car's body and is recessed into the sheet metal of the all-steel body.

Back in the 1960s, you just weren't cool if your show car lacked a heavily padded dash, so the original owner of the car must have been the coolest cat on the block.

Although fully street legal, the car is powered by a 354-inch Chrysler V-8 complete with a Weiand 6-71 blower and a pair of Edelbrock 500-cfm carbs.

The hand-fabricated front cowling hides the radiator from view and really brings a touch of the 1960s to life. Tiny PIAA lights lead the way at night and are barely visible inside the maw of the cowl.

A throwback to the heyday of hot rods is the 14-inch Halibrand Sweet Swirl wheels that were polished before being mounted with M.T. rubber. A Corvette leaf spring bridges the gap between the rear wheels which carry drum brakes and another set of Halibrand Sweet Swirl rims. A Currie nine-inch rear end carries 3.50 gearing and is tied into place by a Posie four-bar system. As might be expected, all suspension components have been treated to chrome plating.

The chosen motor for the car is the exciting Chrysler 331 Firepower Hemi block that displaces 354 cubic inches. The 354 heads are joined by a milder grind cam to deliver plenty of power now that the car is driven from place to place. A matching set of Edelbrock 500-cfm carburetors get their mixture force fed to the motor through the Weiand 6-71 blower that sits on the block.

This belt-driven beast makes a sound that is not easily mistaken for anything. It also makes big horsepower when the pedal is squeezed. The air intakes are pure retro, hailing from the 1960s and looking right at home in 2006. The Zoomie headers are another bit of nostalgia, and are hand made bits from High Speed Welding. Each tube holds Power Pulse discs within their walls to quiet the motor a bit and to tame exhaust travel. Fuel is drawn from a 10-gallon Rock Valley fuel tank by an electric fuel pump, delivery to the hungry mill. The resulting power is transferred to a Chevrolet Turbo 400 gearbox holding three speeds within the case.

Open either door of the car and you are immediately sent back to a time when vinyl was cool and padded dashboards were all the rage. A set of newer Pontiac Fiero seats have been upholstered in white and purple by Schober's Trim and Upholstery. The curvaceous and well-padded dashboard was built in 1961, but was recovered to match the fresh seating in 1998. Puhl's House of Kustom was the purveyor of such things and many more when this car was first built.

Seen between the spokes of the Grant steering wheel are Auto Meter gauges and an original Sun tachometer. The Genie shifter is replete with a chrome skull shift knob and Billet Specialties was tapped for the gas and brake pedals. A complete Pioneer sound system is inside, plus electric windows with the glass tinted for comfort.

Exterior lighting is LED in the back, with PIAA lamps housed in custom 1948 buckets up front.

Despite its 30-year nap in Texas, the car looks as great as ever in its new colors and updated trim. Let's face it, a classic hot rod will always be a classic, regardless of what the calendar tells us.

With the roof chopped four inches, the resulting window dimension also changes radically. The small chrome grille helps to hide the required third brake light from view when not illuminated.

Hand-shaped for this car, the vintage-looking Zoomie pipes each carry three Power Pulse discs within their walls to help quiet the otherwise thunderous music that would be produced.

BARON'S 1954 CHEVY

Owner: Bill Baron
Builder: O'Connell Specialties

With a penchant for all kinds of hot rods, and a long-standing interest in the '54 Chevy, Bill Baron decided to combine both worlds and have one car to fit his impeccable tastes. While, 1955, '56 and '57 Chevrolets may be far more popular, we think the result of hotting up a 1954 is something truly unique. With O'Connell Specialties doing the conversion, we knew the finished car would be perfect.

In its stock configuration, the body of the '54 Chevy is a bit dowdy and certainly not all that sleek. Wanting a car that looked as good as it was powerful, major changes were made to alter the outer shell. This created a far more appealing visual package. Tim O'Connell's first step was to remove all the exterior trim pieces and factory door handles. To open up the look of the car's profile, the small vent windows were removed and one-piece glass was substituted for the multi-pane arrangement.

Smoothing out the front end somewhat, a set of Jeep Liberty headlights was used in lieu of the factory Chevy units. The front fenders were then crowned and the new headlights were laid back at a more relaxed angle. Additional smoothness was achieved by filling in the hood seam and by adding a one-piece bumper to the front end. Custom parking lights and a custom grille assembly completed the work at the leading edge of the '54. A single-piece rear bumper was also installed, along with custom taillamps.

When choosing paint for his Chevy, Bill decided to keep it in the family and went with 50th Anniversary Corvette Red and Super Silver, with mica chips added for flair. Separating the two colors and replacing the original chrome spears are hand-painted graphics from Jim Ross of Letters and Lines. His work contains all the detail of the original hardware, while keeping the lines of the body free of clutter. Smoke gray tint was added to the new glass to complete the sinister nature of the car's new look.

This '54 Chevy is not simply a pretty car with no spine. It is packed with power under the revised hood. In 1954, the biggest engine you could order in

With styling cues from the early days of the Corvette, the resulting cockpit is a blend of old and new with plenty of comfort for up to four occupants.

Even packed with Rockford Fosgate power amplifiers, the trunk has plenty of carrying capacity for those weekend-long car shows.

Virtually screaming "Corvette," the console is a one-off piece by O'Connell Specialties that was packed with high-end gauges and electronics.

A Nissan donated the front bucket seats. They were then reupholstered by Schober's Trim in a burgundy leather and Ultrasuede combination.

Talk about screaming, the four exhaust ports beneath the rear single-piece bumper make a quick exit for departing fumes.

Doing nothing more than looking good, the hood ornament was taken from the outside of the car and mounted in the engine bay.

your Chevy Bel Air was an in-line-six that produced a meager 125 ponies. In keeping with his desire to go fast while looking good, Bill swapped the tired old mill for a much newer motor that would serve his needs.

Now squeezed into the rails of the '54's frame is a Corvette LS1, 5.7 liter V-8. Adding more fuel to the fire is a Magnason supercharger and intercooler bolted to the top of the already healthy mill. Stainless steel fuel lines draw life from the custom aluminum tank that holds 25 gallons of high-test gasoline in safety.

Sanderson exhaust headers lead to a polished, 2-1/2-inch diameter system complete with Magnason stainless steel mufflers. It all exits the rear of the car through a set of four large, round chrome ports. This is definitely not your father's Chevrolet. The big motor draws breath through twin K&N air filters that in turn pull their supply through a custom air intake tube, finished in chrome, of course. A Viper fan helps to keep things in the right temperature range, as does the Be-Cool aluminum radiator with a custom shroud. The Chevrolet four-speed gearbox, complete with overdrive, sends the power to the rear end via a carbon fiber driveline.

Suspension for the '54 was taken from a C-5 Corvette. It was narrowed 6-1/2 inches in the front and 4-1/2 inches in the rear before being fitted with an air bag suspension system to adjust ride height at will. When bringing the car to rest, Bill hits the button and

drops the car onto its haunches. It looks very sinister indeed. More Corvette hardware is found in the disc brake and wheel department. Z-06 rims are mated to Dunlop SP900 rubber at all points, leaving a firm footprint regardless of the surface.

With all that style outside and matching power under the hood, Bill wanted an interior that went along with the theme. Taking a clue from the early Corvettes, Tim crafted a sweeping console to hold the gauges, radio controls and shift lever in a style that was fitting of the car. The top of the console is semi-circular in design, much like the dash used on the first series of 'Vettes.

The stainless steel insert panel keeps the bank of Classic Instrument gauges in a tidy array with the Pioneer AM/FM/CD unit just beneath. The radio head is connected to some very powerful Rockford Fosgate amplifiers located in the trunk. Keeping the atmosphere comfortable, no matter what the velocity, is the Vintage Air system for heat and air conditioning. Power windows and Nissan seats covered in leather and Ultrasuede complete the driver and passenger section of the tour, while a custom shaped rear seat coddles the occupants there.

It should be fairly obvious by now that when Bill Baron decides to build a car, he leaves no stones unturned and no detail behind. Turning to Tim O'Connell to apply his range of talents ensures Bill that the outcome will be every bit as cool as his vision.

When he parks the car, Bill drops it down on the air-controlled suspension so it has a stance that looks much like an animal ready to pounce.

FLAMED '34 FORD FIVE-WINDOW COUPE

Owner: Jeff Kuhn
Builder: NA

When Jeff began the build a 1948 Chevy pickup project, it was taking far longer to complete than he imagined. His patience to complete the truck to his exacting needs was not an issue, but having no hot rod to drive around in was. To fill the void until his truck was complete, he found this 1934 Ford to keep him happy. The '34, five-window coupe is an icon in the universe of hot rodding, and one with black paint and a flame paint job tops the list of classics.

Assembled on a Roadster Shop chassis, the car rides on a beam axle in the front and a Pete and Jakes setup in the rear. Wilwood, four-piston disc brakes are attached to the front spindles while drum units are mounted to the rear. A Ford nine-inch rear end takes orders from the General Motors five-speed manual gearbox with a floor-mounted lever. American rims of the five-spoke variety are polished and ride with Goodyear rubber under each of the flowing fenders. Sprouting from the front suspension are a pair of "S"-shaped bumpers that would do little in the event of a crash, but look great anyway.

The roof of the car was chopped by 3-1/2 inches for a more rakish appearance and classic stance. The flip-out front windshield allows fresh air to flow in when opened and is the only method of cooling the occupants while driving. The proud front grille remains in its factory chrome finish and the painted hood is perforated with louvers for added engine cooling. Suicide doors are used for

The tailpiece of the car is augmented with its own set of louvers, as well as blue-dot taillight lenses and a simple fuel filler neck.

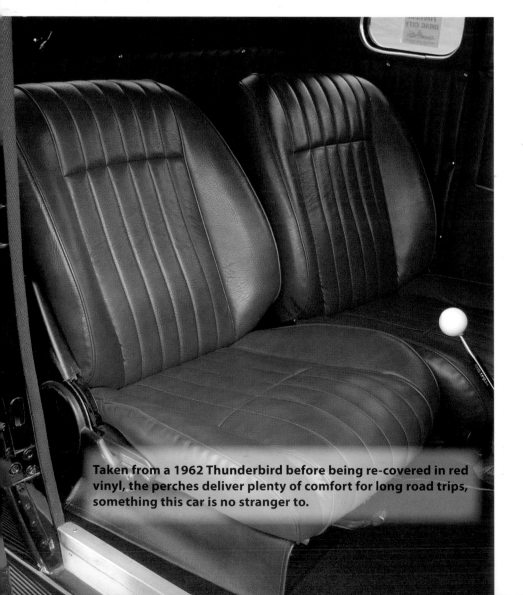

Taken from a 1962 Thunderbird before being re-covered in red vinyl, the perches deliver plenty of comfort for long road trips, something this car is no stranger to.

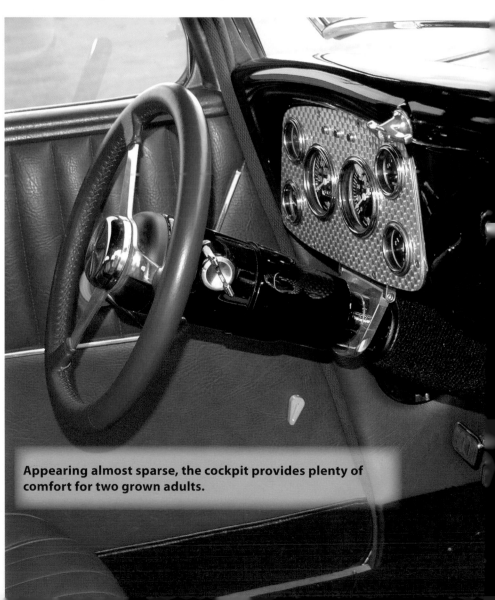

Appearing almost sparse, the cockpit provides plenty of comfort for two grown adults.

A turned-metal panel from SoCal is packed with Stewart Warner instruments to keep the driver up to date on vital stats.

Doing things the old fashioned way, the gearbox is "rowed" by grabbing the cue ball shift knob and selecting the required ratio.

Five-spoke American rims are all the car required in the way of flash. Anything more would be over the top in a '34.

another bit of nostalgia. They have blacked-out hinges.

Speis Hecker paint was applied in a shade of basic black with traditional flames running from front to back. The yellow to orange licks are tipped in red and outlined with bright blue for a true old school appearance. The sweeping tail section of the '34 is slotted with more louvers, a pair of teardrop-shaped taillights (complete with blue dot inserts) and the stand-alone fuel filler neck.

Lurking beneath the flamed and louvered hood is a 420-cubic-inch aluminum Chevrolet block with Edelbrock cylinder heads. The

naturally-aspirated mill is fed by a tripleheader of two-barrel carbs. To heighten the curb appeal of the engine bay, the bodies of the deuces have been painted red, and sport ribbed K&N covers cast in aluminum. Fuel lines are polished, as are many other items on the small-block motor. An electric fuel pump brings the required liquid to the intake from an Aeromotive fuel tank that lies between the rear frame rails. A Griffin aluminum radiator keeps things from getting too hot and factory GM pulleys hold the belts in place.

The interior of the car is done simply, with plenty of attention

The wide fenders, tall grille and large diameter headlights are all original Ford gear, while the flame paint job adds a touch of hot rod.

to detail. A pair of seats from a 1962 Thunderbird has been re-upholstered in bright red vinyl, as have the inner door panels and roof liner. The boot of the floor-mounted shift lever has also been wrapped in matching red vinyl to complete the ensemble. A three-spoke steering wheel sprouts from the painted dash and is trimmed in red vinyl, accenting the interior's theme. A cue ball shift knob adorns the end of the chrome lever for show and comfort. Having a manual gearbox beneath the floor requires frequent use of the shift mechanism, so convenience plays a role in the design.

A turned-metal dash insert from SoCal is packed with contemporary Stewart Warner gauges. A Kenwood audio system provides music on command and the peaceful nature of the engine's exhaust note doesn't require a lot of volume.

The headlights are taken directly from a 1934 Ford with the tail-lamps coming from a 1939 model of the same make.

Although Jeff's truck took longer than planned to complete, this beautiful Ford carried him through, and remains in his garage alongside the silver Chevy pickup.

Three deuces are trimmed in red, and topped off with aluminum K&N caps for a finishing touch.

1967 CHEVY NOVA TWO-DOOR WAGON

Owner: Bill Jelinek
Builder: Route 66 Motorsports

In the day-to-day operations of Route 66 Motorsports, Bill will occasionally trip over a car that ends up in his work area. After buying this 1967 Nova, his only plans were to spiff it up, then sell it to another buyer.

As the car sat in his shop, the idea crossed his mind to change it from a four-door wagon into a two-door model, much like the mid-'50s Nomads from Chevrolet or the 1964 and '65 Chevelle 300 two-door wagon. With this idea in mind, the shop went to work converting the shell and removing two of the previous portals. In typical fashion, Bill and his crew decided not to do things halfway, and soon found themselves completely immersed in building a high-end show car.

With a clear objective now in sight, a long list of changes had to be addressed on the body of the car to meet the two-door plan. Every hint of factory trim, including emblems, handles and moldings, were shaved from the sheet metal. This left much cleaner shell in its wake. The upper sections of the doors were created from scratch to fit the revised body line, and internal door latches supplanted the unsightly factory units.

The rear bumper was smoothed and filled, before being frenched into the updated body. The front bumper was also shaved and filled to match the sleek profile of the rear. Once satisfied with the alterations in the contours and configurations, a blend of PPG Harlequin Essences paint resulted in the Blue Amethyst hue that now glistens on the car's body.

Hidden beneath the new and improved body lies a factory undercarriage that was also modified to accept some enhanced running gear. The struts are empowered by a fully-controllable air ride system with a set of General Motors disc brakes behind the Billet Specialties GT67 wheels. The rear suspension has also been fitted with air ride control allowing Bill to drop or raise the car at will, depending

Antique Auto Meter gauges reside in a modern billet panel that is attached to the hand-formed dashboard, which is painted in the same Blue Amethyst as the body.

The air ride controls and electric window switches are hidden from view until the lid of the armrest is opened.

Not something seen in too many hot rods, this wagon is stocked with a pair of real back seats to carry two friends along to the shows.

The ribbed and molded lining used in the storage section of the car extends onto the rear door, allowing easy loading and unloading of weekend gear.

Nearly completely hidden from view by the handmade cowling, a 350-cubic-inch Chevrolet crate engine lies in wait.

on whether he's driving or showing the car. A matching set of Billet Specialties GT67 rims fit snugly beneath the rear wheel wells and Nitto rubber was used under each fender. Another set of GM disc brakes adorn the rear wheels, bringing the total to four rotors for plenty of stopping power.

Power for this enhanced grocery getter is a 350-cubic-inch crate engine from Chevrolet. The 350 horsepower total was coaxed from the block with normal carburetion and a bevy of additional hot rod tricks. The engine is largely hidden from view by a custom-fabricated shroud that is painted to match the exterior and trimmed with accenting graphics. The balance of the engine bay has been shined up with plenty of gleaming trim and chrome goodies. A Be Cool aluminum radiator is seen along with chrome pulleys for the final touches of form meets function. A Turbo 350 transmission is bolted to the back of the V-8, delivering three speeds to the driver.

Inside the car we find a raft of handmade components and glove soft leather. The seats are from a 1999 Chevrolet Monte Carlo cut down for use in the wagon. The entire upholstery job was tackled by Ogden Top & Trim. Just behind the wrapped shift lever we find two alloy handles that function as door releases. Opening the lid of the hinged armrest reveals controls for the air ride suspension and electric front windows.

All glass is now tempered and tinted, and the rear panes have their own switches in the back seat. Hardly a common sight in the hot rod arena is a set of usable seats in the back. The bucket style seats are capable of carrying two adults in comfort. Behind those buckets we find another completely functional area that can be pressed into service carrying any nature of objects. The molded, ribbed floor lining extends onto a rear door that drops down for easy access to the load space.

A custom-shaped dash is fitted with a billet trim panel holding Auto Meter Antique gauges in place. A GT Series wheel from Billet Specialties complements the interior and matches the wheels mounted to the outside of the car. A hidden, yet fully capable sound system, is controlled by use of a remote for great sounds without clutter.

Though his original plans were to simply sell this '67 Nova, Bill's the outcome earned Bill the ISCA Custom Championship award in 2003/2004 in the Eastern division. I'd hate to see what would have happened if he'd set his sights on winning from the beginning!

Changing from four-doors to two required fresh sheet metal on the doors, and all-new, fitted, tempered glass.

1967 CHEVROLET CHEVELLE

Owner: Ryan Harrington
Builder: Getz's Hot Rod Innovations

Here we see another case of an innocent restoration gone nasty. When Ryan first got the car, he envisioned returning it to a completely stock configuration, with fresh paint, interior and engine. When his friend Terry bought himself a Nova drag racing car, he offered Ryan the rear axle out of it. This simple act of innocence changed the direction of Ryan's intentions, and he then created the monster we now see here.

At the core of this beast is the 502-cubic-inch crate V-8 that has been heavily massaged by Getz's Hot Rod Innovations to achieve its current output. The '67 Chevelle from Chevrolet had a few potent engines on the option sheet, but even the mighty 427 they sold pales in comparison next to the lump under, and sticking out of the car now.

Individual throttle bodies feed each of the eight cylinders with electronic fuel injection controlling the flow. A 10-gallon, race-legal fuel cell resides in the trunk. Gas doesn't last long with heavy use of the pedal. Eight K&N air cleaners are housed in four individual aluminum cages, and the entire bank rides high on the motor, requiring an open hood for clearance. Several hot rods in this book feature hand-bent exhaust tubes, and this Chevelle runs with 2-1/2-inch diameter pipe from header to tip, allowing a clean getaway for errant fumes.

The headers themselves are heat coated for better heat dispersion and longevity. Massive billet valve covers hide the monkey motion in the motor and are machined to match the surfaces of the air cleaner housings. A T400 transmission sends the three speeds to a nine-inch Ford rear end for final take-off.

The contours of the 1967 Chevy have remained unaltered, but all extraneous metal trim has been removed and replaced by air-brushed graphics. Even the "Chevrolet" "Super Sport" and crossed flag emblems have been applied in painted form, adding some flair

Pneumatic lifts hold the trunk lid open in its new configuration.

Even when it's open, the reflective panels on the underside of the hood allow glimpses of the big engine.

Squeezed between the rear tubes of the roll cage is a single seat that is limited in comfort, but looks great anyway.

A tasteful blend of billet, vinyl and custom components creates a livable space that is also race-ready.

Once the deck lid is open we can see the myriad of hardware stored within. The fuel cell, audio amplifiers and battery boxes are all trimmed to accentuate the rest of the car.

and cleaning up the appearance. The front and rear bumpers are also color-keyed to match the crème color applied to the lower section of the body, while Candy Apple Copper covers the top half.

Custom sheet metal alterations include a trunk lid that opens from the right edge versus the usual hinge point, and the suicide hood. The opening in the hood facilitates the passage of the eight air cleaners, and mirrored panels under the hood reflect the tremendous amount of effort taken to create the motor. Along with the 10-gallon fuel cell in the trunk, we find a pair of matching battery boxes, complete with billet covers. A pair of PPI audio amps is mounted to the front wall of the boot, and two of the roll cage tubes also protrude into the space. Sections of billet, machined to match that used in the cockpit, make another nice detail on this well-done race car for the street.

The cabin of the Chevelle is a functioning combination of safety, comfort and electronics. A set of Carillo bucket seats are fitted with full, six-point racing harnesses, and a single rear seat is found in the back. The extensive roll cage takes up a lot of the usual space in the interior, but keeps the chassis stiff and the occupants safe.

Getz cleverly got around the obstacle of having to climb over the side tubes of the cage when entering and exiting the car with a system that slides the side rails into place when the door closes. When the door is opened, the cage sections slip effortlessly toward the front, allowing easy escape. A set of heavy-duty receivers catch the door tubes when the door is closed, completing the integrity of the cage. Not only does the system work, but it's painted to match the exterior of the car, making it a statement of style too.

Some additional billet details are used to dress up the rest of the inner door panels for a complete look. The balance of the cockpit is finished in crème-colored vinyl to match the exterior paint, and yards of billet trim have been added to continue the theme found elsewhere in and on the car.

The custom-crafted dashboard carries Auto Meter gauges and a full compliment of race-required instruments. A Billet Specialties steering wheel is wrapped to match the crème vinyl of the seats, console and doors. Powered by the PPI amps in the trunk, a Kenwood receiver and Kicker speakers provide plenty of volume inside the car.

The chassis of the Chevelle is mostly stock, but the rear end has been tubbed to accommodate the 15-inch-wide Sportman rear tires. A four-link suspension provides plenty of traction when the loud pedal gets pushed and disc brakes haul it down from speed. Up front, drop spindles are attached to the stock axle with coil-over shocks smoothing out the bumps. Colorado Custom rims are covered with B.F. Goodrich rubber under each fender well.

Although not the car that Ryan had originally planned on building, the results of the three-year process are self-evident and very fast.

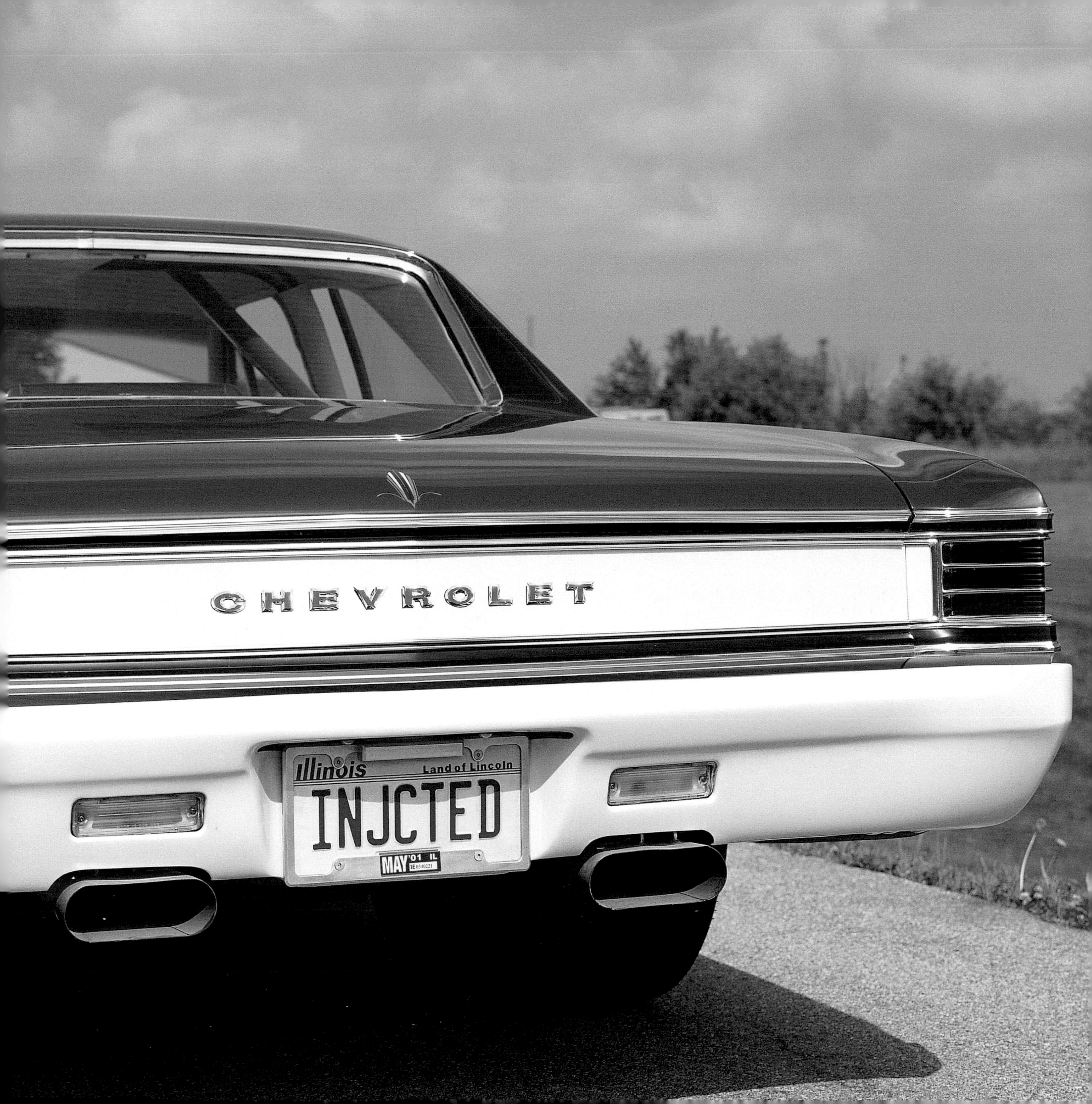
CHEVROLET
Illinois
Land of Lincoln
INJCTED
MAY '01 IL

1957 CHEVROLET CONVERTIBLE

Owner: Mike Harrington
Builder: Getz's Hot Rod Innovations

Before Mike purchased this '57 Chevy, it had languished in storage for 24 years. As most car guys can attest, the 1957 Chevrolet Bel Air is an icon in the car world, whether it's been hot rodded or not. Wanting to add one to his stable, Mike bought the car, and then held it for two more years as he waited for the new Getz's shop to open its doors. Once they were back in operation, the car went under the knife and received a major rebuild.

Having been in dry dock for almost 30 years, there were obvious condition issues that needed to be addressed, so Mike chose the hot rod path instead of returning the car to its pristine factory appearance. Nearly every inch of the body was removed and altered before going back on the chassis. The hood was "nosed," meaning the OEM chrome bits were stripped off, and the trunk was "decked," achieving the same result. All four fenders were revised, which gave the car a slightly different profile without losing its identity as a classic. Roof supports were also lowered, giving the car a more aggressive stance. Under the hood, custom panels were formed to clean up the engine bay. Similar work was done to create smooth inner panels for the front fender wells. Once the sheet metal work was completed, the painting began. Numer-

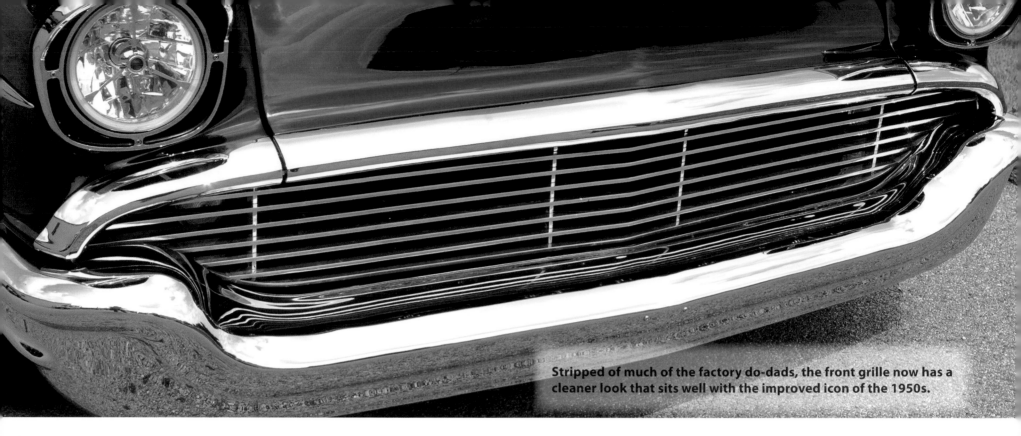

Stripped of much of the factory do-dads, the front grille now has a cleaner look that sits well with the improved icon of the 1950s.

Covered in the same Chrysler Blue and Purple Pearl Essence hue as the body, the sleek dashboard is a model of subtlety. Running from stem to stern of the interior is this custom console, holding a variety of controls and two drinks in their place.

With the key in the "off" position, we find no gauges in the hand-made steel dashboard of the car.

When the key is switched to the "on" position, this bank of Dakota Digital instruments slowly flips into view.

Billet Specialties was chosen as the provider for the billet rims as well as the steering wheel mounted inside the car.

Another bit of craftsmanship from Getz's is the fabricated trident air cleaner system that holds two K&N air filters in place.

All of the car's style and creature comforts can be enjoyed by four full-grown adults with enough room for long days on the open road.

ous layers of DuPont Chrysler Blue blended with Purple Pearl Essence were sprayed on, clear-coated and rubbed to the deep, lustrous shine we see here.

Under the gleaming body is a stock Chevrolet chassis, fitted with revised suspension components at both ends. Fat Man independent front suspension is now on duty for more precise handling and the Heidt's independent rear suspension includes two coil-over springs at each wheel for greater weight handling capability. As expected, every inch of the modern components have been chromed and polished. Wilwood disc brakes slow the car from all four corners, with Billet Specialties wheels bolted to the hubs. The 18-inch hoops roll up front with 22-inch "Dubs" in the rear. The use of contemporary wheels on a vintage classic really makes a statement, and has become quite popular today.

Power for this modern icon is a 350-cubic-inch Chevrolet crate engine that produces 355 horsepower. Fuel delivery is managed by an electronic fuel injection system, complete with the boost gained from the Ram Jet equipment. The trident-shaped air cleaner that sits atop the engine was created from scratch by Getz's Hot Rod Innovations, and uses one of the pointed, rubber tips formerly found on the front bumper guards.

A pair of conical K&N air filters keeps stray debris from entering the engine. Flowmaster mufflers are mounted to the Getz's stainless steel exhaust that exits under the rear bumper of the car. A full compliment of chrome pulleys from Street Performance help to doll up the engine bay and keep the belts in their place. A 700R4 gearbox is married to the motor and is complete with overdrive for comfortable highway use.

When the soft top is dropped and stowed, we get a clean look at the amazing interior of the car. With the roof gone, we get an unimpeded view of the mostly hand-built cockpit.

The first thing you notice is the lack of any instrumentation on the custom steel dashboard that stretches from door to door. This dilemma is corrected as soon as you turn the key. With the ignition activated, a small, rectangular panel of gauges flips out of the smooth dash, and is packed with Dakota Digital instrumentation. Turn the key to "off" and the panel recedes from view once again.

Another Getz trick is the console that runs from the dash to the back seats. The café of the unit is trimmed in billet and holds an array of goodies in its polished face. Controls for the A/C and heat from Vintage Air, as well as the Alpine audio unit, electric window switches and even a two-slot cup holder, are included in the blend. The console rides between seats taken from a 1996 Dodge Intrepid. The seats were upholstered in ultra leather by Mike Bell at Custom Tops & Interiors. A Billet Specialties steering wheel has skin to match the seats and the standard billet spokes and hub.

Once the work began, it took more than three years to complete this upgraded classic from Chevrolet, but it turns heads no matter where it's driven, making the time and effort worthwhile.

1929 FORD MODEL A "TIN MAN"

Owner/Builder: Brian "Tin Man" Limberg

With extensive exposure to the hot rod universe as a kid, Brian learned a lot from watching his dad bang stuff into shape. When he was a bit older, he began to work alongside his father, and with this hands-on training, he began to compile extensive background on building a car from the ground up. His efforts and talents eventually landed him jobs at two highly respected hot rod shops, the latest being Getz's Hot Rod Innovations. His title of "fabricator" is well deserved, and this custom of his own design is proof positive of his skills.

Although he was highly capable of building this car from scratch, money was one stumbling block that he needed to overcome. Even this minor setback would not be enough to deter him from building the car of his dreams. Working slowly, and with materials at hand, he set off to fabricate his signature vehicle. His work in the metal forming field earned him the nickname "Tin Man" and that moniker was applied to the car as it came to life.

He learned from his father the proper way to set up a chassis, so that's where his initial efforts were applied, using nothing more than 1/8-inch flat stock for the curved rear portion of the frame and two 2 x 4-inch mils steel for the rest. The flat stock was cut into a horseshoe pattern. Then, using small sections of steel, he welded the metal to follow the contour of the curve. This box section frame rail would provide him with a dropped seating position that falls between the sides, not on top.

The body was created by welding a skeleton of half-inch steel into the general shape he desired. Then he formed individual sheets of steel or aluminum that were attached to the skeleton, resulting in a solid, three-dimensional form. A variety of power hammers, steel shaping machines, and good old-fashioned sweat equity was employed to create the subtle curves, each with a purpose.

Several of the sections were based on a 1929 Ford's dimensions, but were formed by Brian for use on his car. With his design carrying the driveshaft alongside the driver's ribcage, safety was also an issue that he addressed in the assembly. Several hoops of steel were employed to reinforce the drive shaft tunnel that runs through the center of the cabin. This keeps the occupants safe from flying debris in the event of a driveline break. The radiator cowl was purchased from a vendor, then sectioned and revised to meet with Brian's design.

The side panels of the three-piece hood were given relief dimples to provide adequate clearance for the exhaust headers. Once the body panels and frame were completed to his demands, DuPont paint was used to cover the smoothly sanded steel and aluminum. The silver hue is the same used by Daimler-Chrysler to paint their steel wheels, and a heavy layer of clear coat was used to bring more luster to the finish.

The tiny roof panel is another work of magic from Brian's mind It flips backwards on custom hinges to provide entrance and escape from the interior. Black Harts cloth covers the exterior surface with silver lining, complete with Brian's "Tin Man" logo covering the inside of the lid. A small pair of latches secures the roof when going down the road and provides quick release when access is needed.

The suspension is another mix-and-match proposition, with every component the result of Brian's knowledge and desire. The 1940 Ford front axle and spindles are joined by 1948 Ford backing plates and finned brake drums from a Buick. A 1946 Ford donated the shocks that were rebuilt before being installed. A straight rear axle from a 1940 Ford was suspended by adjustable shocks and a trailing arm was hidden inside the bodywork. A second set of Buick finned drum brakes were added to the back for added stopping power. Six-teen-inch wheels from a 1946 Ford are used at all four points, with period "dog dish" wheel covers.

Financial restrictions forced Brian to drive the car sans interior for a year. Once he had enough resources saved, he contacted Schober's Trim and Upholstery to cover the minimal, yet deeply sculpted seat cushions in silver and black vinyl.

The dash is more of Brian's handiwork, and is fashioned after a

Although styled like a 1932 Ford, the car's dash was hammered into shape by Brian's own hands and carries Stewart Warner gauges, but no radio is in its expanse.

Brian drove the car for a year with no seats but we prefer the cozy two-place arrangement that was eventually installed.

Hinged at the rear, the roof opens up with a simple touch and allows Brian and a passenger to climb in and out of the car.

Its origin is unknown, but this massive set of headlights throws a decent amount of light onto the streets at night.

1932 Ford model. Set into the old-school dash are modern Stewart Warner gauges, but no audio system of any kind. The triple-spoke steering wheel slips off of the hex-end steering shaft for easier access to the driver's seat. The front windshield is the only glass you'll find on the car, with no side curtails or rear closure in the hinged roof.

Power for this diminutive roadster comes from the Chevrolet 283 engine fed by a trio of 94 carburetors. The Edelbrock manifold holds them all in position and is painted black to accompany the ribbed valve covers that were installed. Each 94 carries a modified SoCal Frog-Mouth scoop complete with K&N filters to keep the incoming air free of dirt. The engine sips fuel from a custom-formed tank that hangs over the driveshaft like a saddle.

Exhaust is kept to a minimum with more hand-crafted parts that include the heat-wrapped

megaphones with large diameter turnouts. A total lack of mufflers makes a livable level of racket, but make it clear why a radio wasn't installed.

It required more than four years to complete, but Brian's end product is something he can certainly be proud of. With 95 percent of the car being handmade, and of his own creation, we certainly won't see another one crossing our path anytime soon.

Somewhere a 1940 Ford is laying around without an axle as Brian saw fit to transfer it to the rear end of his own hot rod.

Hand-formed exhaust megaphones are attached to the end of the straight exhaust pipes and do little in the way of sound deadening.

1957 CHEVROLET STEP-SIDE

Owner: Bob Parks
Builder: Getz's Hot Rod Innovations

It took him two decades to reach, but Bob Parks achieved his dream of one day owning a customized '57 Chevy pickup. He had always admired the truck's style and had visions of what his own copy would look like long before driving this one home. Having waited 20 years to do the build, he knew exactly what he wanted and where he'd turn to have the work completed. His knowledge of Getz's Hot Rod Innovations and their longstanding reputation for building award winning customs made his decision of where to take his truck a snap.

Getz's didn't earn their reputation by squirting paint onto untouched car bodies, so they took out their finest steel cutters and went to work on Bob's '57. Some 2-1/4 inches were chopped from the roof, and 1-1/2 inches were removed from the profile of the hood, resulting in a more rakish wedge shape. The roof's sun visor was extended by 1-1/2 inches and was blended into the roof panel to become a seamless line.

Side vent windows were removed completely, as were the outside door handles. The Step-Side rear fenders were also truncated. Now a revised tailgate rests between rounded bed corners. Under the hood, which now opens in suicide style, we find a smoother firewall and curved fender panels. In the cockpit, the factory dash was retained, but all extraneous shapes and trim were removed, leaving a glassy-smooth surface behind.

Once satisfied with the alterations to the steel, DuPont Cin-

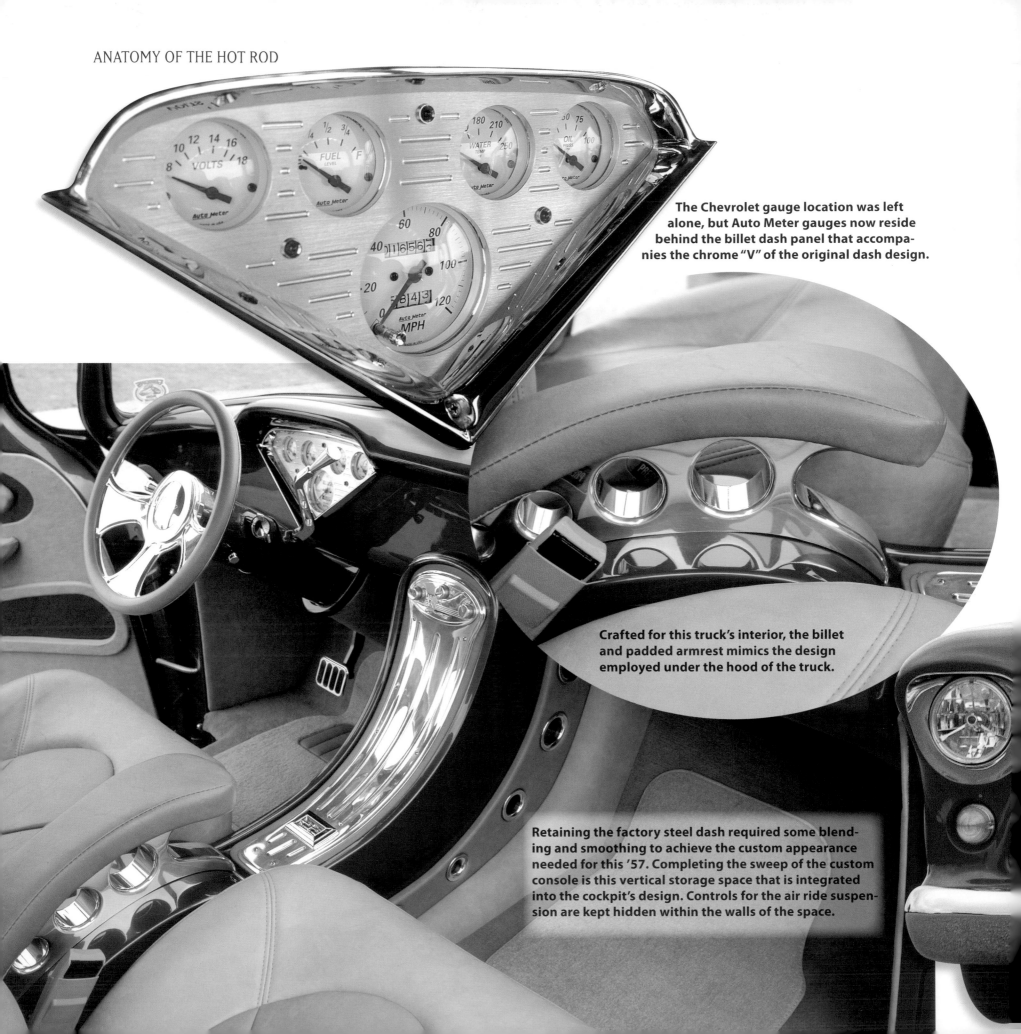

The Chevrolet gauge location was left alone, but Auto Meter gauges now reside behind the billet dash panel that accompanies the chrome "V" of the original dash design.

Crafted for this truck's interior, the billet and padded armrest mimics the design employed under the hood of the truck.

Retaining the factory steel dash required some blending and smoothing to achieve the custom appearance needed for this '57. Completing the sweep of the custom console is this vertical storage space that is integrated into the cockpit's design. Controls for the air ride suspension are kept hidden within the walls of the space.

The inner bed of the truck has been treated with as much care as the outer shell, and the wood and stainless trim glisten when the electric cover is opened.

Cleansed of much of the factory clutter, the front grille now sports a much tidier appearance along with the "Cin Bad" logo painted onto the chrome bow tie.

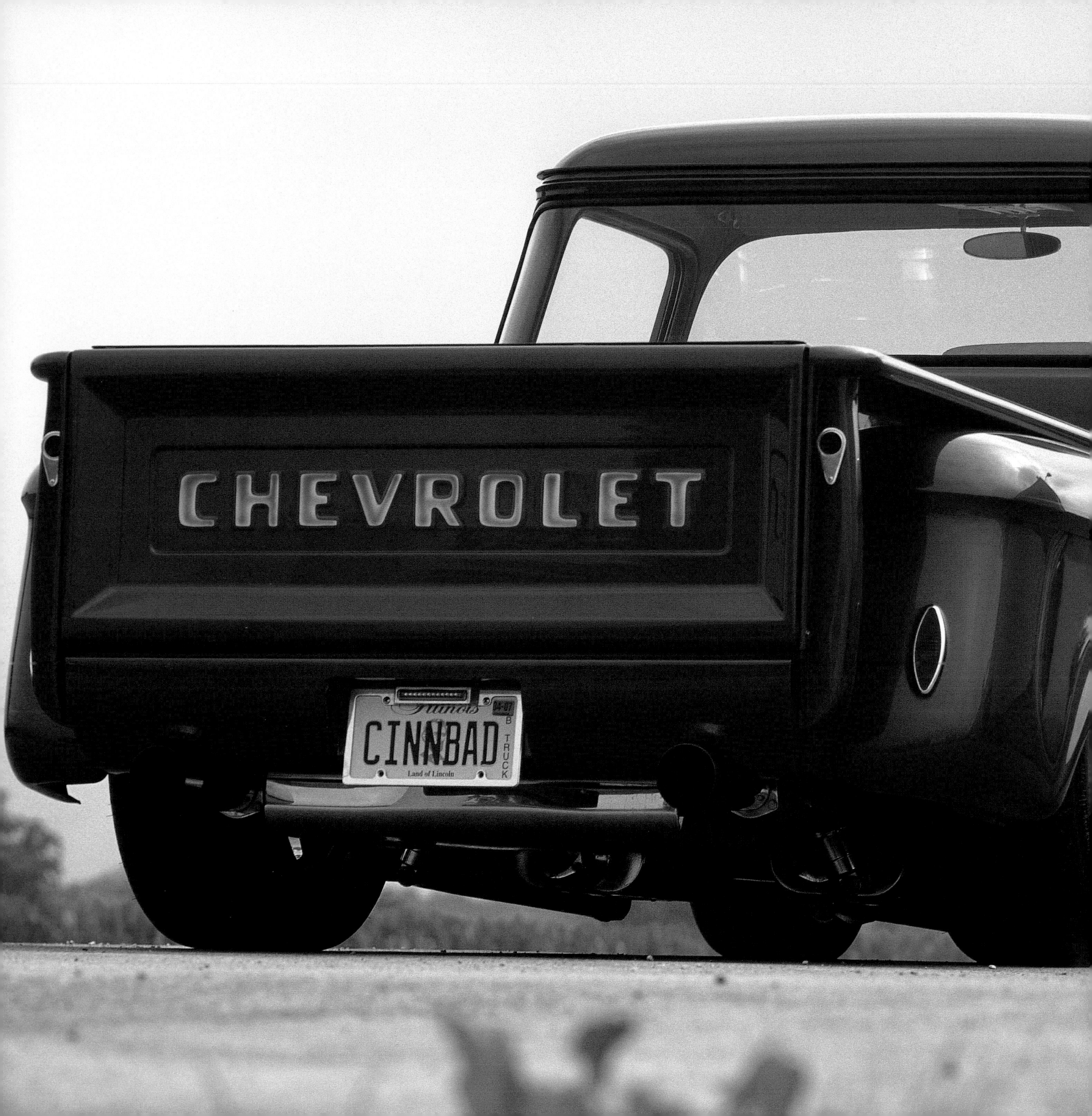
CHEVROLET
CINNBAD
Land of Lincoln
TRUCK

namon was sprayed onto every inch of the steel, followed by clear coat and lots of wet sanding. The finish was then rubbed out to achieve the flawless glow it carries. The chosen hue was partially responsible for the "Cin Bad" moniker applied to the truck, and we are about to learn about the other reason.

Opening the fortified hood of the truck reveals a beautifully sculpted aluminum air cleaner housing that was created just for this '57 by Getz's. The eight cylindrical ports draw in fresh air to feed the brace of 750-cfm Holley carbs that lie beneath. Just to the south of the carburetors we find a Weiand 8-71 supercharger, which forces the fuel and air mixture into the engine under pressure for a greatly enhanced performance curve.

All of this action is applied to a 400-cubic-inch Chevy small block that has been bored to .30 over stock. Street Performance pulleys are finished in chrome and a Griffin radiator plus auxiliary electric fans provide more than adequate cooling. The exhaust system was hand-bent using stainless steel tubing and passes through a pair of Flowmaster mufflers before making the final departure near the rear bumper. A General Motors 700R4 transmission sends the three speeds, plus overdrive, to a Ford nine-inch rear end that also features Positraction.

Alterations to the exterior of the Step-Side also include frenched turn signals in the front, cat's-eye taillights in the rear fenders and a custom bed cover that opens and closes at the touch of a button. The front grille was also trimmed of some of the factory flash for a cleaner look.

What we can't see is the Heidt's independent front suspension complete with air ride control and the four-link rear suspenders, also with air ride.

Hitting the buttons housed in the cockpit drops the truck down onto its wide expanse of rubber when at rest, creating a truly menacing stance. The 12-inch power disc brakes can be seen behind the American Racing wheels used under each fender. The 18-inch rims roll up front with 20-inch hoops out back. B. F. Goodrich G-Force T/A radials provide the grip and control.

The cabin of this altered '57 is equally complete and no stone is left unturned. The power adjustable bucket seats are upholstered in two-tone leather of sand and parchment hues. The dash, smoothed of all factory trim, holds a team of Auto Meter gauges in the original gauge cluster, now held by a billet panel.

The console between the seats is another show of applause for Getz's shop. The sleek contours begin at the dash, then flow backwards between the seats where they are completed by another vertical section that opens up to reveal the air ride controls. The billet and padded armrest carries the same theme as the multi-port air cleaner under the hood and gleam in chrome.

Vintage Air provides the hot and cool conditions with the control panel mounted at the top of the curving console. An American Racing steering wheel, wrapped in matching leather, falls into the driver's hands in a relaxed, adjustable position. A Panasonic sound system has its speakers hidden behind the seats with only small puncture wounds in the leather to belie their position. The cabin is enclosed with custom windows from Pro Glass are tinted and of the safety glass variety.

It took 3-1/2 years to complete the truck, but having waited 20 to even begin, Bob can't complain too loudly about the length of the process. He loves the results and we're sure the truck will garner awards wherever it's taken.

1934 FORD FIVE-WINDOW COUPE

Owner: Tony Kroll
Builder: Route 66 Motorsports
**   and Al Johnson**

Harboring a long-standing desire to own a hot rod that stood out from the crowd, Tony selected a classic 1934 Ford, five-window coupe, then veered off the classic path when choosing his color. Wanting to avoid subtlety entirely, he reviewed hundreds of color charts and catalogs, ending up with the House of Kolor's Hot Pink Pearl hue that screams off the car. With this decision made, the rest of the build could commence, and Route 66 Motorsports was tagged as the lucky builder.

The project came to life with a 2 x 4-inch steel tube frame that was outfitted with Mustang II independent front suspension. Wilwood disc brakes joined in on the hunt along with a pair of Billet Specialties GT93 wheels in 15 x 7-inch size. The aft end of the chassis carries a 12-bolt rear end fitted with 4.56 gearing and hydraulic shocks.

Assuming you can get past the audacious hue of the car, many of the major components are not as exotic as some we've seen, keeping the cost and complexity down. Tony wanted a car that he could drive anywhere without hesitation, and the hot pink monster has yet to let him down with mechanical failure. Two more Wilwood disc brakes on the rear axle roll behind a larger set of Billet Specialties GT93 wheels measuring 17 x 8 inches. Goodyear Eagle tires are spooned on all four rims for their durability and long life.

Back on the surface, the primary body of the five-window coupe is steel with its handles shaved and filled seams for a smooth exterior. The fenders and running boards are fiberglass, joining the two worlds into one seamless concept. The width of the running boards necessitated the application of the rubber covers to avoid damaging the

The steel dash has
been augmented by billet inserts,
and a bank of VDO gauges tells Tony all he needs to know.

Looking the part of the factory original, the tall, vertical grille assembly was custom crafted for Tony's '34 Ford.

Billet Specialties was chosen as the supplier of the alloy wheels and they are wrapped with Goodyear Eagle tires.

Quick Silver

An all-steel body is joined by lightweight fiberglass fenders that combine style with modern convenience.

The Quick Silver shift mechanism is linked to the turbo 400 gear box that is mounted under the floor, and makes lightning-fast gear changes a breeze.

The stainless steel exhaust travels the length of the car and terminates with these massive chrome outlets.

KROLL 34
03-07

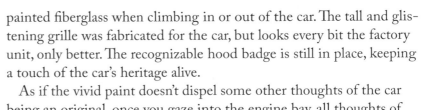

painted fiberglass when climbing in or out of the car. The tall and glistening grille was fabricated for the car, but looks every bit the factory unit, only better. The recognizable hood badge is still in place, keeping a touch of the car's heritage alive.

As if the vivid paint doesn't dispel some other thoughts of the car being an original, once you gaze into the engine bay, all thoughts of yesteryear are lost. The biggest engine offered by Ford in 1934 was a 221-cubic-inch V-8 that produced 85 horsepower at the crank. These numbers do not equate when building hot rods, so a 350-cubic-inch Chevrolet engine was slipped between the rails and claims a 350 horsepower rating.

A single Edelbrock 650-cfm carburetor sits atop the manifold, and it draws breath through an oval air cleaner with folded filter. While the rest of the cramped engine bay bristles with good-looking billet trim, the basic motor configuration is again built for speed with dependability. A high-zoot injection system paired with exotic cams may produce more power, and look really cool, but try finding parts when you're in Podunk, Tennessee.

As it's built, the car makes plenty of power, and Tony is pleased with how quickly it can jump from a standstill. A turbo 400 gearbox was tweaked with a shift kit and manual valve body, and is rowed by a Quick Silver shift on the floor of the interior. A hand-bent stainless steel exhaust runs the length of the chassis and is only punctuated by a set of Flowmaster mufflers. Large diameter exhaust tips protrude from just under the rear bumper and tell the hot rod crowd you mean business.

Opening either suicide-mounted door of the coupe reveals an interior that boasts both comfort and convenience, along with a dash of the same brilliant pink hue we find on the outside. The steel dash is covered in Hot Pink Pearl and fitted with a billet glove box door, electronic and dash panel. VDO gauges tell Tony all he needs to know about the vital statistics as he gazes through the spokes of the Billet Specialties Flame steering wheel.

The central-mounted billet panel holds the Jensen radio along with an HVAC vent and control knobs. A large, easy-to-read tachometer from Auto Meter hangs just below this cluster and tells the driver what rpm has been reached with only a glance. Other accoutrements include power windows with a rear unit that drops out of sight for better circulation. Power locks and a tilt steering column bring modern comfort to this '34 while the custom seats, covered in a muted gray leather, provide plenty of comfort for a driver and passenger.

All in all, Tony is satisfied with his Hot Pink Ford. The car performs to his standards and certainly doesn't go unnoticed when he rolls into the local cruise night. I suspect the car would stand out on the Las Vegas strip, but that's just how he wanted it.

1939 FORD

Owner: Bill & Debbie Jelinek
Builder: Route 66 Motorcars

Spending a major part of each week building customs and hot rods, Bill Jelinek's wife Debbie is exposed to all sorts of exciting vehicles. After seeing so many cars roll in and out of the garage, she told Bill it was time for him to build one for her. With his goal of always making his customers happy, he started to draw up the plans with Debbie to satisfy her demands. One of her desires was to have a car painted in a bright hue. She scanned numerous color charts before settling on the vibrant green that now covers the body. The color seemed to compliment her personality, as well as that of the car.

After many discussions about the make and model of her hot rod, the '39 Ford was selected as the winner. As soon as the remaining build parameters were agreed upon, work began.

Coast To Coast was chosen as the provider of the tubular chassis on which the car rides, and it provides a multitude of options as to what running gear can be mounted to the corners. Constructed from a combination of round and rectangular sections of steel tube, rigidity is paramount. A Heidt's Super Ride II system was polished before being bolted to the front cross members with Wilwood disc brakes providing the anchorage. The rear suspension hails from a Corvette C-4 in its entirety. Wilwood brakes were again used on the aft axle to ensure confident braking from any velocity. Chicayne Softlip wheels from Billet Specialties were bolted onto all four hubs with 17 x 8-inch models used for each rim. Nitto 455 series rubber, 205/40/17 up front and

Boasting 350 horsepower, the GM crate engine is well dressed in billet and its own screaming green accessories.

With turn signal bulbs built into each of headlight lenses (far right), and a hand-made grille (right), the leading edge of the car draws attention as soon as it appears.

Playing the part of a vintage '39 headlamp, the modern versions carry brighter bulbs and integrated turn signals.

Mounted to the Coast To Coast dash is this billet bezel that holds the Auto Meter gauges in an easy-to-read configuration.

With its three-spoke design to mimic the Chicayne wheels from Billet Specialties, the hoop was wrapped in leather to match the seats.

Lifted from a Fiero, cut down and modified for use, the bucket seats are covered in leather for comfort and style.

larger 245/40/17 on the rear, delivers plenty of traction with a quiet ride.

The rear tires are pressed to their limits of adhesion when Debbie applies too much pressure on the gas pedal, bringing the 350-cubic-inch General Motors crate engine to life. Producing 350 horsepower using only natural aspiration, the car is quick off the line. A single carburetor is responsible for the delivery of the fuel and air blend, and sits atop a polished manifold.

Polished billet hardware abounds under the hood, and what doesn't shine is trimmed in an equally outspoken green. Exhaling through a hand-bent 2-1/2-inch stainless steel exhaust system, the final wisps of vapor exit through a single outlet that is centrally located beneath the tail end. Flowmaster mufflers are installed to quiet the rush of fumes as they race towards their solitary exit port.

Bolted to the rear of the crate engine is a General Motors turbo 400 transmission that has been upgraded with a shift kit and 2800-rpm stall speed. Each of the three speeds is selected with the floor mounted Lokar shift lever in the cockpit.

One of the many features of this car is the lift-off Carson top. Basically a hard top that is crafted to appear like a convertible,

it lifts off in one swift motion once two simple latches are released. The name refers to the original shop that created the concept, and they have become a staple of the hot rod universe.

With the top lifted and set aside, we get a much clearer view of the tidy cabin. A set of Pontiac Fiero seats were first cut down in size, then were modified for use.

Custom leather hides cover the altered saddles in a muted tone that contrasts strongly with the energetic Hot Green Pearl applied to the body panels and dash.

A tapered center console gently falls from the dash to the rear of the cockpit, and is also trimmed in leather on the upper surfaces. A triangular bezel carved from billet aluminum is located in the center of the dash and holds an array of Auto Meter gauges in its portals. The dash itself is another product of Coast To Coast and in this case was sprayed to match the exterior. The matching Chicayne pattern steering wheel from Billet Specialties is bound in matching leather to complete the ensemble. A tilt steering column, power windows and hidden Auto Sounds audio system are included on the build sheet and make the car as drivable as it is attractive.

Hardly able to overlook the vivid Hot Green Pearl paint, we find a body that has been shaved of all exterior badges, handles and moldings, resulting in a seamless form. Suicide doors are examples of more custom alterations, as is the grille that was created at Route 66 Motorsports for the car. The final color was achieved by blending several hues of PPG paint into the shade and intensity that suited the car and the owner.

Only eight months were required to build Debbie's '39 Ford, but her husband Bill has had plenty of practice building high-end hot rods for his clients, making this example just one of many that have rolled through the doors of his shop.

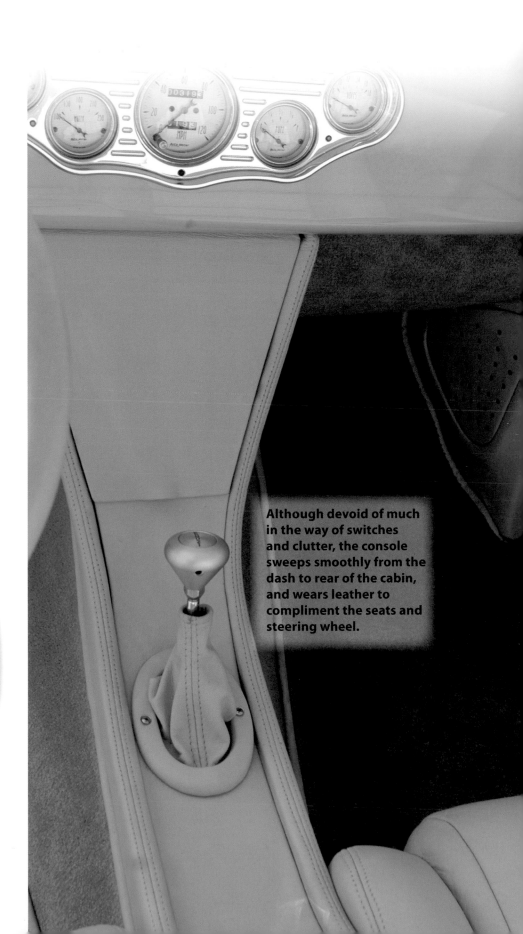

Although devoid of much in the way of switches and clutter, the console sweeps smoothly from the dash to rear of the cabin, and wears leather to compliment the seats and steering wheel.

1946 FORD DELUXE

Owner/Builder: Dick Gatz

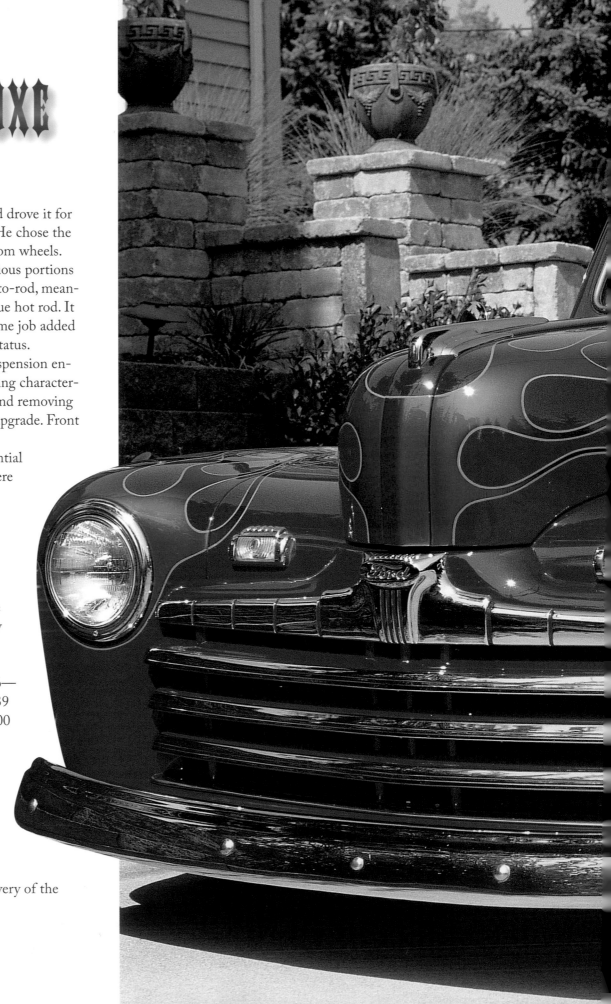

Dick bought this 1946 Ford at a show in 1995, and drove it for two years before doing any modifications at all. He chose the step-by-step plan and started by adding the custom wheels. Bit by bit he changed, improved and re-built various portions of the car. In the middle of the process it became a resto-rod, meaning it wasn't stock, but wasn't radical enough to be a true hot rod. It was a decade later, in 2005 when he had the classic flame job added to the paint scheme, and crossed over to true hot rod status.

The big coupe rides on its factory frame rails, but suspension enhancements were made to improve the ride and handling characteristics. Slipping the front suspension from a '74 Nova and removing three inches from the width would become his latest upgrade. Front disc brakes were from the same '74.

The Ford's rear axle was fitted with a 10-bolt differential with 3.08 gearing. A pair of 1974 Nova leaf springs were introduced to add some added travel to the assembly. The same poor Nova also lost its rear drum brakes to Dick's project. Wanting to keep an air of classic in his build, he chose Halibrand Sprint wheels, complete with three-legged, chrome knock-offs in their centers. He used 15-inch diameter rims at all four points with six-inch-wide units up front and seven-inch under the rear fenders. Goodyear Eagle RS-A rubber is currently mounted on the car, although he had run with wide whitewalls for a spell.

Ford offered buyers two power plant choices in 1946— an inline 226-cubic-inch six or a V-8 that displaced 239 inches. Even the bigger of the two only cranked out 100 horsepower, so Dick knew he'd need to up the ante if he was going hot rod. The original motor was pulled and a 350-cubic-inch Chevrolet crate engine went in its place.

With an Edelbrock 650-cfm Performer carburetor handling the fuel dispersion, he now turns out about 250 ponies, a far more respectable number. Hotter spark is provided by the MSD electronic ignition and an electric fuel pump provides unbroken delivery of the precious fluid.

In place of the 1946 vintage tube radio, a modern Alpine AM/FM/CD unit now provides the music.

Something old and something new is in the interior, and a Lecarra steering wheel sits at the end of a tilt column.

Retaining the factory contour and much of the chrome, the revised dash carries all new gauges within the original openings.

Both front and rear bench seats are the same as installed in 1946, but a tasteful combination of parchment and sand dollar vinyl now covers the acreage.

Another bit of nostalgia is the 1946 hood ornament that still resides on the crest of the hood.

The final step taken before reaching official hot rod status was the application of the multi-colored flames.

Another blast from the past is the stock taillights that still protrude from each of the fat rear fenders.

Factory chrome strips still adorn the lid of the trunk, and the license plates defer to the car's dimensions that hardly are svelte.

A Moon billet air cleaner is joined by valve covers of the same material, and almost every visible surface on the mill has been polished. An increased diameter exhaust, now measuring 2-1/4-inches, runs under the chassis and passes the fumes through a set of Flowmaster mufflers. A turbo 350 transmission provides the driver with his choice of three gears and the shift kit adds sharpness to every gear change.

The interior of the car is another fine blend of vintage and modern, bringing new levels of convenience to the tried and true layout. The seats remain in their 1946 form, but are now covered in a combination of parchment and sand dollar-colored vinyl. Schober's Trim & Upholstery was chosen for the interior work, and they have outdone themselves again. The factory dash is largely intact, but a raft of modern toys now graces the curving surface. An Alpine AM/FM/CD unit resides in between two VDO circular gauges in the original Ford ports. Another four-gauge display sits directly in front of the driver's view. It also holds modern VDO gauges in the factory Ford locations.

A tilt steering column adds another touch of modern world convenience, as does the Lecarra steering wheel. The wheel is wrapped in vinyl to match the bench seats.

The last step taken before the car reached official hot rod status was the application of the wild flames over the Sikkens Chevy Apple Red paint. To achieve the level of depth and color shift the process featured multiple layers, beginning with a silver and gold base coat. Over that went on five different hues to build the color to what it is now. The colors used to reach the vibrant flames were as follows: Oriental Blue, Cobalt Blue, Purple and Violet. The outline of the final flames was done in Process Blue by "Jive" and makes the perfect finishing touch.

Being an automotive technician by trade, Dick knows his way around a shop, and did most of the work on the car himself, turning to the experts for paint and upholstery only. It took him a decade to complete, but every step was worth the effort.

A lot of Dick's hot rod remains as it was in 1946, with only fresh paint to spruce things us. The chrome grille and bumper are carryover parts from the original car.

1939 CHEVROLET SEDAN "THE OUTLAW"

Owner: Rich "Pyro" Pollack
Builders: Rich Pollack & Marvin Leigeb

Rich Pollack makes his living as a Chicago firefighter, and in an effort to compensate for the time spent running into flaming buildings, he builds some very cool cars and motorcycles. The time that he's on duty, but not battling fires is often used to hand-craft components for whatever he's building at the time, and the results are always amazing. His two-wheeled machines have earned him numerous spots in national magazines and taken home countless trophies. In the Windy City, there are times when riding a motorcycle just isn't practical, so "Pyro" decided to build something that provided a roof over his head for those cooler months of the year.

The decision to build a hot rod was fairly simple, but choosing what car to begin with wasn't as easy. He wanted something a bit off the beaten path and definitely wanted to avoid the billet rods that litter the landscape. Finding a solid 1939 Chevrolet sedan, his mind was set on what car to use as the platform for his own flavor of hot rod.

The two-door sedan of 1939 was by far Chevrolet's most built body style, but oddly enough, they are as rare as hen's teeth today. Over 300,000 were assembled for the model year, but Rich hadn't seen one for decades when he stumbled onto this one. He had been on a weekend road trip when he spied the car resting in a barn in Michigan. Striking a deal with the owner, the car was hauled home a short time later and the work began. There are some who might restore a rare survivor like this '39 to its former condition, but Pyro ain't one of them.

Modifications to the body are mild, yet make the car a true hot rod. Shaved door handles, frenched-in taillights and a two-inch boost to the width of the rear fenders made up the list of steel modifications. The original hood was discarded but had been a part of the vehicle when located. The Chevrolet chassis still rides beneath the body, but a few extra cross members were added for strength.

Wanting more power than the '39's inline-six could deliver, Pyro and Marvin put together a Chevy crate engine that now pumps out plenty of energy. Mounted on top of a single velocity stack is this air cleaner from a 1959 Cadillac. Generous amounts of pinstripes add some flair to the otherwise mundane bit of hardware.

The painted dash, filled with modern Auto Meter gauges, along with a raft of vintage trim, makes for a real contrast of the ages.

Like opening a portal into the past, many of the interior components are carried over from the original car along with lots of upgrades.

The original grille was retained from the '39 two-door sedan and now helps to conceal the headlights that lurk behind the intricate strips of chrome.

Although he disdains the "billet rods" that are seen in every corner of the globe, Pyro did use a set of billet pedals in the interior of his car.

Front dropped spindles of the Mustang II variety came from Heidt's with Ford Mustang disc brakes behind the front rims. Chassis Engineering was selected for the slider springs utilized in the rear, along with a sway bar for improved handling. A pair of drums from a 1960 Thunderbird helps to slow forward progress. Chrome reverse rims at all four corners are wrapped with Coker Classic 15-inch rubber for that gangster look. Hey, we said Pyro lives in Chicago. The altered ride height and wide whitewall tires really change the attitude of the car, and not in a friendly kind of way.

Power in the 1939 Chevy would have been produced by an inline-six that put out a whopping 85 horsepower at the crank. Any hot rod builder worth his salt knows that a number that puny will only get you laughed at, so Rich and his buddy Marvin built a slightly larger

mill to be installed. Beginning with a Chevy 350 block, they bored, stroked, ported and polished until an improved 355 cubic inches was attained. To ensure longevity, Ed Pink connecting rods hold TRW pistons where they belong, regardless of the rpm being achieved.

A solitary 600-cfm Holley carburetor pulls the flammable fluid from a Harwood fuel cell located in the trunk, and is fitted with a velocity stack and 1959 Cadillac air cleaner. A pair of Hooker Super-Comp headers begins the exhausting process of venting exiting fumes, and a 2-1/2-inch stainless steel set of tubes does the rest. Stainless Specialty mufflers do what they can to quiet the rambunctious motor's noise levels. Four speeds can be selected using the mile-high shift lever in the cockpit, and it's attached to a Muncie "Rock Crusher" gearbox. A nine-inch Ford rear axle, fitted with 3.90 gears, sends the

power to the rear wheels and Positraction handles the details.

The spacious interior of the car is a direct throwback to the heydays of hot rodding, complete with Torch Red vinyl upholstery covered with a vividly colored blanket from South of the Border. The front saddle is actually from a Chevrolet S-10 pickup while the rear was purloined from a Dodge Caravan before being wrapped in the violent red vinyl.

The steel dash was modified by the removal of the glove box door and ashtray. Then pinstriping was added in copious quantities. Auto Meter gauges rest in the factory ports and a vintage 1950s steering wheel allows control. The heater and fan are still carryover units from 1939 and keep the car's interior toasty during the cold Chicago winters. A 4 x 8-foot pane of gray tinted glass was cut to size

before being installed in every window opening. Previously fender-mounted headlights now dwell behind the horizontal bars of the '39 Chevy grille, and the car lacks any rear indicator lights.

Once hauled home, it took Rich and Marvin about two years to complete the project, and their pal Larry Grobe sprayed on the "barn-fresh" paint. Designed to look old and weathered, it is actually modern hues applied in a method that looks decades old. The final touch was the classic flame job that decorates each side of the car. Whether it's his height of 6' 8", his shaved head or simply one of his cool customs, people are sure to notice Pyro regardless of how hard he tries to stay under the radar. Naming the Chevy "The Outlaw" was Rich's way of telling the world what he thinks of his four-wheeled creation.

Along with the "barn-fresh" paint job, Larry Grobe applied a panel of cool flames to each side of the car, making sure that Pyro remains visible.

Rich made a hinge that often draws stares of admiration from viewers and other hot rod builders.

1928 FORD TUDOR

Owner: Tom & Debbie Styczykowski
Builder: Getz's Hot Rod Innovations

Ten years ago when Tom thought it would be fun to build a hot rod that would be great to drive, he had no idea of how many dips in the road he'd experience during the process. Overall he said the process was not what he'd expected, but in the end the car was just what he'd wanted from the beginning, making it all worthwhile. Starting from scratch does have its drawbacks, but is still the only way some people choose to build the hot rod of their dreams.

A combination of 2 x 4-inch steel along with 1-3/4-inch chrome-moly tubing was used to create the chassis beneath the car's body. Dan Smith was chosen as the man to handle that portion of the build, and it proved to make for a stable platform for the remaining components. A Total Performance straight axle was paired with a four-bar setup and dropped by two inches for a low stance in the front.

Wilwood disc brakes were added to the mix along with Colorado Custom wheels. Goodyear Eagle rubber rolls on the front rims. A four bar setup also holds the polished Winters alloy nine-inch rear end in position and Wilwood brakes were selected again. Five-spoke Colorado Custom wheels also grace the rear fenders with B. F. Goodrich Radial T/A tires out back.

Peeking behind the custom-crafted alloy hood vents you get a glimpse of the 350-cubic-inch Chevy engine that dwells within. Opening the handmade hood gives us a much better look at the tri-power arrangement that feeds the car. Each individual carburetor sports a cylindrical air cleaner with louvers cut into the sides and chrome covering the surface.

The underside of the hood has been painted as carefully as

Helping to reduce the amount of equipment mounted in the dash, the overhead console holds the JVC radio up and out of the way.

Providing a wide range of information, this pair of Classic Instruments gauges does the work of many while saving clutter.

The billet fins were created by Getz's Hot Rod Innovations to provide some distraction to the otherwise open sides of the hood panels.

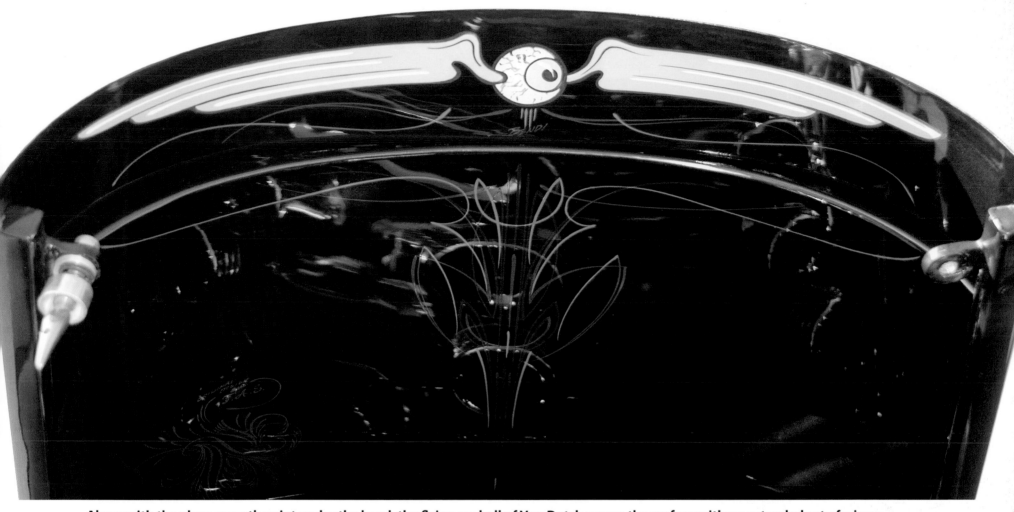

Along with the glass-smooth paint under the hood, the flying eyeball of Von Dutch graces the surface with an extended set of wings.

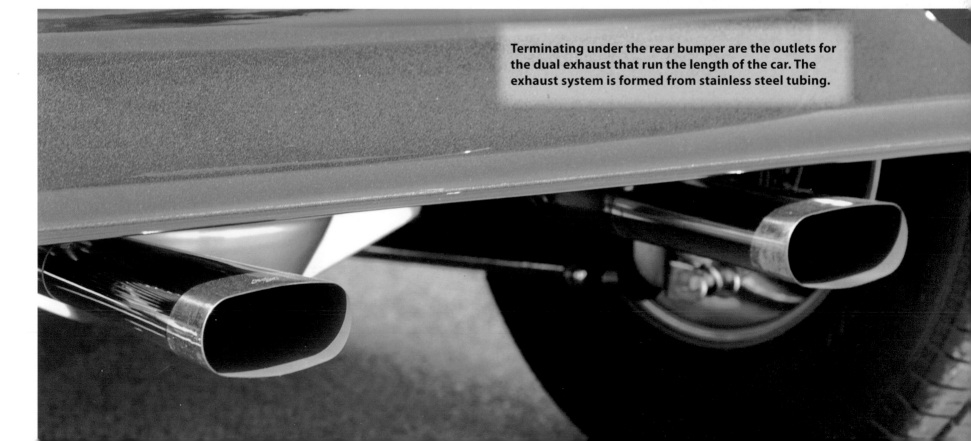

Terminating under the rear bumper are the outlets for the dual exhaust that run the length of the car. The exhaust system is formed from stainless steel tubing.

the outside and is complete with elongated flying eyeball graphics and a bevy of pinstripes. Braided stainless steel lines complete with anodized fittings to keep the engine bay tidy and avoid leaks under pressure. A 350 turbo gearbox with a 2,800 rpm stall speed was bolted onto the motor and sends power to the Winters rear end through a General Motors drive line. A full-length dual exhaust flows from the engine to the rear bumper and is 2-1/4-inch stainless steel through-out. Smittys mufflers tame the volume to a healthy degree.

The all-steel body was highly modified for use and the most obvious change is the 2-1/2-inch chop the top received. The front visor was molded into the roofline to enhance smoothness as well. The front fenders and running boards were rolled as one component and flow smoothly to the chopped and tubed rear fenders.

The roof of the Model A was filled in with steel, adding a high level of stiffness to a car that was originally powered by an inline four cylinder engine that pumped out a whopping 40 horsepower. The new Chevy mill produces far more than that, thus it needed a much stiffer body structure. A one-piece rear splash apron cleans up the appear-ance of the view most people get of Tom's car. Taillight housings have been integrated into the curves of the fenders for a tidy layout too. Nestled in between the front frame rails we find a billet assembly that allows two high-powered Dietz headlights to throw their light through narrow slits. The car lacks bumpers at either end because Tom didn't want them cluttering up the sheet metal that took so long to perfect.

The three-piece hood was also created from scratch including the horizontal billet grilles that decorate the otherwise gaping openings on each side panel.

Inside the car we find a nice collection of new and old, all wrapped in Ultraleather for comfort. The front seats began their lives in a Pon-tiac Fiero and were cut down for use in the '28. The same glove-soft hides that cover the seats were used to wrap the factory dash. A set of cylindrical gauges from Classic Instruments fill the primary open-ings in the dash and two small knobs give the driver control over the climate control system.

The nearly vertical steering column has some tilt adjustment for added comfort. The wood-rimmed Banjo steering wheel from Grants looks right at home with the leather and billet trim. The molded headliner has also been grafted with a full-length console that holds the JVC radio in its grasp. Tinted panes were installed by Pro Glass to ensure clarity and safety.

It may have taken much longer than Tom had expected to build this car, but the travails were all worth the time in the end. The car is driven on a weekly basis and enjoyed by all who see it rolling into their town.

1940 FORD DELUXE

Owner: John Langston
Builder: (Final) Route 66 Motorsports

Had this 1940 Ford been born as a cat, it would certainly be nearing the end of its nine lives by now. Purchased in 1980 as a "beater" that was to be resold, John decided to make some mild alterations to the car. Once those were completed, he'd sell it for sure. Now, 26 years and about four levels of hot rod improvements later, John has no plans to sell his Ford.

Soon after buying the car, John threw a coat of yellow paint, thin white wall tires and a few more toys into the car while working in his own garage. A small block 283 V-8 was assembled from a variety of existing engines before being slipped into the rails of the chassis. Another $5 was spent acquiring the Chevy Vega bucket seats that were bolted to some 2 x 4-inch lumber. The car was driven for three years in that condition, with a fresh coat of yellow lacquer and some candy pearl flames added to the exterior.

In 1985, the car was stripped of its yellow color and repainted with black enamel. The chassis was also blasted free of the previous paint before being replaced with a fresh coat of black. Interior upgrades included a set of mohair upholstery, molded dash and fresh gauges.

The car stayed in that condition until 2002 when John made the decision to go big time with the appearance and performance of the '40 Deluxe, and turned to Route 66 Motorsports to accomplish the desired alterations.

Upon its arrival at Route 66, the body was pulled free of the chassis and everything was again stripped to bare metal. The newly naked frame rails were boxed for strength as John had plans to upgrade the engine as well.

In addition to the frame rail augmentation, Chassis Engineering components including the front cross-member and sway bar were thrown into the mix. Split wishbones, Posie's reverse eye spring

Stewart Warner Stage Three gauges now reside in the Ford's steel dash that was stripped of all the excess grille work and smoothed before being painted.

Steel wheels painted black are complimented with 1948 Ford "dog dish" wheel covers and 1951 Mercury trim rings.

As seen from the outside, Route 66 cut 112 louvers into the steel hood to let some of the crate engine's heat escape.

The car was driven for years with a home-built 283, but John's 2002 reincarnation resulted in bolting a 350 crate engine into the stiffened frame rails.

A Lobeck's four-spoke steering wheel is mounted to a GM tilt column for added convenience when driving the car.

The white interior is a mixture of two shades of white marine vinyl, outlined with gray piping.

Adding to the flair of the stock body are the yellow, orange and blue flames that lick the hood and fenders.

Some 112 louvers were cut into the hood to let the sunshine through and heat out.

The Ford chevron taillights are still in their stock form, but now carry brighter L.E.D. bulbs within the chrome housings.

Unaltered in their physical dimensions, the nose and grille of the '40 Deluxe are now treated to bright paint and the leading edge of the flame paint.

and Super Bell I-beam axle were then assembled. Disc brakes from Posie's along with GM calipers do the braking on the front axle and 15 x 6-inch solid wheels are trimmed with '48 Ford "dog dish" wheel covers and '51 Mercury trim rings.

Under the trunk of the car, a 1968 Camaro 10-bolt axle is suspended by a set of Chassis Engineering parallel leaf springs complete with a sway bar and gas shocks. Some 1968 Camaro drums are found behind the 15 x 7-inch steel rims that are also decorated with the same caps and rings as the front wheels.

The previous engine was replaced with a new Chevrolet 350-cubic-inch crate mill that hammered out 300 horsepower. A polished Edelbrock Performer manifold was mated to a 600-cfm carburetor from the same firm. A GM electric fuel pump draws from the factory Ford storage tank. A set of Pro Car headers were coated then bolted to a full-length two-inch aluminized exhaust complete with Turbo mufflers. A Muncie four-speed transmission is shifted with the Hurst floor mounted lever in the cabin.

The earlier mohair upholstery was torn off and replaced by two-tones of white vinyl, trimmed with gray piping. Schober's Trim was again chosen to cover every inch of the car's cockpit, and the German square-weave carpeting was added. The 1940 dash was retained, but was stripped of the grille and excess trim before being filled and smoothed.

The standard glove box was left behind and Stewart Warner Stage Three gauges took the place of the previous instrumentation. A tilt steering column was topped off with a Lobeck's, four-spoke "lake"-style steering wheel. The American car was then accessorized with the finest in German audio with the installation of the Blaupunkt AM/FM/cassette radio into the upper curve of the steel dash. A piece of tinted glass was slipped into the gasket for clearer driving regardless of the conditions.

Exterior lighting up front is produced by powerful Cibie European H3 halogen bulbs. Rear lamps are contemporary L.E.D. units placed into the 1940 housings with Vintique integrated turn signals.

Finishing off the 2002 conversion was the application of the PPG black paint along with the classic yellow, orange and blue flames, pinstriped in a process blue for the final touch.

Through the car's many iterations, John has enjoyed many a weekend touring and showing it, with stares of admiration at almost every point in its history. With John's heavy involvement with the now famous World of Wheels car show each year, his ride has to make a strong statement, and his '40 Ford fills the bill.

1937 PLYMOUTH COUPE

Owner: Matt Delap
Builder: Getz's Hot Rod Innovations

Ask an automotive enthusiast to close his eyes, and then imagine a 1937 Plymouth coupe in his mind. Odds are, if there's any recall that registers, it's of a dumpy car his dad drove that was big, yet lacked much in the way of power. Now imagine his surprise if he were to open his eyes and find this 1937 Plymouth staring him in the face.

Not what most people would expect, and that's just what the owner wanted. Once he had the car of his dreams in his hands he contacted Getz's Hot Rod Innovations to turn it into a reality. The process of turning a lumpy '37 Plymouth into something sleek and powerful is not for the feint of heart, but Getz's experience and talented staff took to the job like a team of experts.

Making a list of the steel alterations that lie ahead, some major styling issues had to be addressed. The original fenders would be reshaped for a smoother contour before being molded into the body's shell. The roof had to be chopped for a sleeker look and many related components would be changed in the process to match the refined shapes. All clunky bumpers would soon be found in the recycling bin with the wide running boards that came on the car.

The new running boards would be one-piece units that flowed from fender to fender and carried one smooth contour throughout their length. The front fenders had to be extended by three inches to accommodate the headlights that were now slanted backwards and mounted deeply into the curved steel. The radiator shell was also reshaped before being fitted with finely cut vertical fins of billet. The two-section butterfly hood of the '37 Plymouth was welded into a solid piece then ventilated for the motor's intake to breath freely.

Once the steel work was complete, the unique silver and yellow paint was applied by Getz's. Instead of the factory chrome trim and flash that were affixed to the car, airbrushed details now surrounded the waistline of the body. Smaller airbrushed details can be found on numerous locations too, really adding a high degree of detail to the finished scheme.

Carrying the silver and yellow concept inside, the cockpit is packed with modern-day toys. The custom dash and waterfall console carry the gauges by Dakota Digital, and an Alpine audio and DVD system complete with a flip-out screen for viewing movies. Sub-woofers and amplifiers are also of Alpine design, and the integrated system produces ample sound whether in movie or music.

The steel dash and console have also been trimmed with the same glowing hues as the outer body and carry their own airbrushed graphics for a complete ensemble. The shimmering bucket seats are covered in a subtle shade of silver and the roof liner was molded to include the sculpted details. An American Racing wheel is hung off of a tilt column for added ease of entrance and exit to the driver's seat. As expected, the steering wheel wears a coat of matching leather to compliment the buckets.

With as much thought and effort as they put into the style of the car, Getz's was not about to leave the stock 201-cubic-inch inline-six under the revised hood.

Taking the place of the Plymouth engine is a 355-cubic-inch Chevrolet block, complete with a supercharger. The blower breathes in through a pair of Holley 750-cfm carburetors and a space age intake.

Upon command from the driver's foot, the two gaping maws of the polished Shotgun intake open wide to suck in all the air the world has to offer. Between the whine of belt-driven blower and the rapid opening of the intake's portals, it's a sight and sound to behold. A Chevrolet 400 automatic transmission is controlled by electric switches in the cockpit, providing seamless gear changes at the touch of a button.

Underneath all this flash and power is a chassis that is mostly stock, but stiffened and fitted with a rear section that is tubbed to allow for the wider rear tires. Heidt's suspension up front holds Wilwood brakes in check. A four-link rear end includes a nine-inch Ford differential and axle with more Wilwood braking components.

American Racing rims grace the B. F. Goodrich rubber under each fender for a classic yet aggressive appearance. A full length dual exhaust makes its exit under the rear body work through a set of chrome trumpets.

The alteration from stock to outstanding took about a year, but the revised Plymouth isn't anything like we see in the old time ads.

Still carrying five windows, the roof has been chopped and altered for a sleeker look to continue the hot rod theme.

The molded headliner adds another dimension of quality to the car and matches the silver cockpit perfectly.

Using nothing but steel, Getz's formed this seamless dashboard before adding the waterfall console and Dakota Digital gauges.

The evil Shotgun intake is the creation of Bill Scoop and menacingly draws in lots of air to feed the powerful motor that lives beneath it.

Although similar in appearance to the stock grille, the revised assembly is sleeker now and carries a toothy grin of billet in its opening.

Replacing the factory chrome and trim with airbrushed graphics carries the custom hot rod theory to the highest degree and the details are life-like in their application.

Hot Rod Source Guide

This listing will lead to you to the fine builders and most often used suppliers in the book.

Billet Specialties
500 Shawmut Avenue
La Grange, IL 60526
800-245-5382
www.billetspecialties.com

Felony Chops 'N' Rodz
1327 B Industrial Drive
Itasca, IL 60143
630-250-8251
www.felonychopsnrodz.com

Getz's Hot Rod Innovations
196 Mill Street
Hampshire, IL 60140
847-683-1956

Heidt's Hot Rod Shop, Inc.
800-841-8188
www.heidts.com

Midwest Hot Rods, Inc
10 East Main Street
Plainfield, IL 60544
815-254-RODS
www.midwesthotrods.com

O'Connell Specialties
2399 Von Esch Road Unit G
Plainfield, IL 60586
815-267-3235

Ogden Top & Trim Shop
6609 Ogden Avenue
Berwyn, IL 60402
708-484-5422

Schober's Trim & Upholstery
744 Montgomery Road
Montgomery, IL 60538
630-585-7912

Route 66 Motorsports
708-997-2277
www.rt66motorsports.com

Expand Your Collector and Restorer Expertise with Help From Hot Rod How-To's!

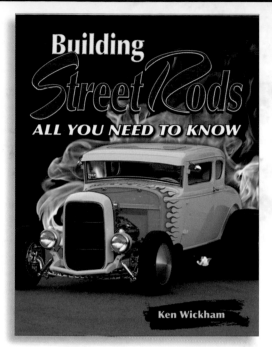

Building Street Rods
All You Need to Know
2nd Edition
by Ken Wickham

Get the guide that gets you under the hood and in the driver's seat of your own cool ride! This easy-to-follow manual outlines practical tip for customizing hot rods, including advice for choosing the right car, handling fiberglass and metal bodies and preventing paint problems. This detailed garage guide is packed with 200 instructional and inspirational color photos.
Softcover • 8-1/4 x 10-7/8 • 176 pages
200+ color photos
Item# SRCB2 • $24.99

Great American Hot Rods
A Full Throttle Chronicle of Custom Cars from the Street, Show and Strip
by Keith Harman, with photography by Chuck Vranas

Feel the power and pull of more than 360 edgy hot rods as you peruse each chapter of this big and bold book. You'll explore a diverse collection of pre 1949 model hot rods, through essential details including basic specifications such as body style, engine and model year.
Softcover • 9 x 12 • 752 pages
360+ color photos
Item# HTRD • $29.99

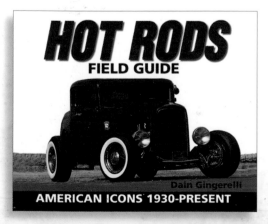

Hot Rods Field Guide
American Icons 1930s-Present
by Dain Gingerelli

Two hundred detailed color photos showcase the toughest hot rods of the 20s, 30s, 40s and 50s, including 1920s-30s modified Model T and Model A Fords, customized '55 and '57 Chevys, complete with captions providing additional specifications about your favorite rods.
Softcover • 5-3/16 x 4-3/16 • 408 pages
200+ color photos
Item# HRFG • $12.99